Living

Outside the Box

United States Copyright Registration #TXu 2-130-395 January 6, 2019

ISBN-13: 978-1092964890

ISBN-10: 1092964894

Paperback copies of LIVING OUTSIDE THE BOX may be purchased in bulk for promotional, educational or business use. Please email hadannahbusiness@aol.com for details

Second Edition: May 2019

Living Outside the Box

Table of Contents

Living Outside the Box

Mission

The mission of the Coachella Valley Economic Partnership (CVEP) is to maintain a focus on the state of the business world, advising the leaders of the Greater Palm Springs, California region on what needs to be done to promote the diversification of the economy in ways that inspire and enable businesses that pay thriving wages to grow or locate in the region.

In the greater Palm Springs region, CVEP is the keeper of the edge and the crafter of the vision for a path to a brighter future.

By fostering entrepreneurship in business sectors such as renewable energy, smart fashion, cybersecurity, the internet of things (IoT), and 5G communication platforms, CVEP grows the region's wealth by driving high wages. CVEP currently manages the Palm Springs Innovation Hub and has been selected as the operator of the Palm Desert Digital iHub.

The thought processes and actions to drive the kinds of actions to bring mega-city technology to a fringe region are addressed in the first 8 chapters. The out-of-the-box thinking and the actions taken to remove intrinsic barriers to entrepreneurial activity that requires ultra-high bandwidth are the subject of Chapter 9, and the final chapter is reserved to share stories about six people who risked it all to live outside the box and change the world for the better.

Living Outside the Box

Living Outside the Box

Prologue

Throughout my career, I have watched corporate executives, boards of directors, politicians, commissions, and committees come together to seek solutions. The concept for this book came about as a result of seeing many of these allegedly purpose-driven meetings result in absolutely nothing new.

The watershed moment when the term "Living Outside the Box" was coined came during my time as the CEO of the Growth Alliance for Greater Evansville when some very specific challenges called for new solutions. Another meeting was about to be scheduled by some members of the executive committee to "think outside the box." My frustrations boiled over at the thought of yet another meeting where the foregone conclusion was that good thoughts would be developed and nothing would be done about them.

From my mouth came the words *"What good is it to think outside of the box unless we have the courage to live outside the box?"* The room went silent. I did not know if I was about to be fired or if my words had struck a nerve, but the next "think outside the box" meeting was not scheduled at that moment.

Afterward, one of the attendees who represented the University of Southern Indiana came into my office; he believed that my statement had been quite profound. His role at USI had been as a facilitator, helping businesses, municipalities, and non-profit agencies engage in outside-of-the-box thinking exercises with hopes that real planning and actions would result. He also expressed many examples of frustrations in cases where little or nothing actually got done as a result of his facilitation sessions. He was so enamored with the phrase "Living Outside the Box" that he did some research to find out if this phrase had been used in the context of a call-to-action following facilitated sessions of "Thinking Outside the Box." Much to the surprise of both of us, it had not.

He began encouraging me to pursue publishing and speaking engagements around the phrase "Living Outside the Box." That was the summer of 2009. It is now 2019 but the phrase and its call to action has never left my mind or my way of living. I work the phrase into every speech that I make whether it is to the Palm Desert Rotary Club, at the annual CVEP Economic Summit, or as the keynote at the Chief Innovation Officers Summit in San Francisco.

The words "Living Outside the Box" always make an impact and I hope it will make one on the readers of this book. As you will see, it is those who take actions that really change the world. Words inspire, perspectives provoke thoughts, but it is only through deliberate actions that progress is made to positively impact the human condition and thus change the world.

Living Outside the Box

The Box

It's so easy when you are thinking inside the box
It's gets a little tougher when you are not
But the problem with thinking inside that old box
Is sooner or later the thinking causes rot

It is so easy to see things the way that they "are"
To see things the way they've always been
But when you do the answers turn out the same
They just lead you to the same old dead end

Have you ever imagined there was no war at all?
If the call was ignored by one and all
If we spent all that money instead creating peace
 The world full of a love so real and raw

Did you ever imagine you'd walk through a wall?
And that you didn't need a door at all
If the answer came to you outside of your own box
Would you be afraid to answer the call?

 Tomorrows a new day doesn't have to be the same
Leave that old box and set yourself free
Stare out at new horizons beyond your four corners
You'll discover a brand new way to see

It's so easy when you are thinking inside the box
When you don't have to do anything "new"
But the truth is you won't make anything happen
Sit there & scratch your head without a clue

Don't you get tired of the same thoughts you have
Of the same old answers you always get
 I think it's time to start thinking outside of the box
Your pay-offs never any good on a safe bet

It's so easy when you are thinking inside the box
It's gets a little tougher when you are not
But the problem with thinking inside that old box
Is sooner or later the thinking causes rot

Living Outside the Box

Living Outside the Box

Introduction

The concept of needing to think outside the box has been around for many years. The box is referring to the status quo or to some standard protocol that is not expected to yield the desired results in a situation that calls for new solutions. Thinking outside the box is often defined as exploring new ideas that are unconventional or looking at problems from a different perspective. Metaphorically "the box" constrains the thought process to things that are already well known and universally accepted. Thinking inside the box does not really require original thought; it only requires sufficient research to understand what is already available to solve any problem that you may be facing.

For example, putting four wheels on a box to make a cart does not require one to think new thoughts or take new actions. About 3,500 years ago, someone invented the wheel. At that time the wheel was not used for transporting goods or people: wheels were used to make pottery. The advent of the wheel as a repository for a lump of clay that could be made into a precision vessel by rotating the wheel was an example of thinking outside of the box and then taking the actions required to realize a benefit. It took roughly 300 years for the wheel to be attached to a box to make a chariot. In reality, it took a weapon of war to inspire the innovation that turned the rotating wheel into an instrument of transportation. Here we are 3,200 years later and all of our ground-based transportation still uses the wheel as the rolling support for platforms of transportation. The automobile, trains, Segways, scooters, skateboards, covered wagons, goat carts, surreys, combines, golf carts, motorcycles and little red wagons for children all use the wheel to facilitate transportation in pretty much the same way the ancient warriors did.

Incidentally, it took roughly 3,100 years after the integration of wheel and box to make a chariot for motorized transportation that moved faster than a horse and rider.

The concept of hovercrafts that use compressed gas to maintain an air gap between hover craft itself and the sidewalk or street came from science fiction, and has been demonstrated in labs and in some water-based applications. Hovercrafts are definitely an invention that came from thinking outside the box that was followed by living outside the box and making one that works. You might say life imitated art as it often does. Will the hovercraft ever become a dominant form of transportation, displacing the wheel, and if so, will it take 3,000 years as it did to go from a horse-drawn chariot to a horseless carriage? Transportation is a prime example of a situation where both thinking and living outside the box have resulted in a legacy of machines that are much easier and more efficient than walking.

Humans Love Boxes

When it comes to boxes, it is of concern just how much humans like boxes and how conditioned we are to migrate to safe places without risks or disruptions. People are conceived and grown inside of our mothers in a sheltered environment that is form fitting and provides all warmth and nutrients necessary to grow into an infant. At birth we are removed from our nice warm

11

womb (our first box), we scream until someone takes mercy on us and swaddles us into our new box which comes in the form of a blanket. Our next box is our bassinet or baby bed: a rectangular box designed to constrain our movements and protect us from falling to the floor and being injured.

At some point babies become toddlers and begin to crawl or walk. Mobility is a freedom that toddlers enjoy and this is the time in life when we all start to test our boundaries and often resent the confines of our next box which we know as our room. Our room is a safe place but it is also a place that restricts movement. Some toddlers rebel against the calm serenity of their room. Some parents make the room a form of punishment by telling children to "go to your room" when behavior is – let's say – a little outside of the box.

As life progresses most people find jobs that have restrictions associated with location, activity, mobility, and the office phenomena called the cubicle, which is nothing more than a box without a top. The easy path in life always seems to be one that is well defined and substantially constrained. Many people will at times find themselves in what we affectionately call a "rut," which is figuratively nothing but a grave with the ends knocked out of it. To humans, boxes provide certainty and comfort the way a kennel comforts a dog.

Finally, at the end of life, we are rewarded with the ultimate box that we all know as a coffin. Then we are put into another box called a vault and lowered into the earth in an earthen box that we call a grave. Is it no surprise that we gravitate to our boxes, finding it uncomfortable to think outside of the box and downright terrifying to live our life outside of the box?

There are people among us who do think and live outside of the box. They are called innovators and their goals and aspirations are as narrow as seeking their fortune and as broad as changing the world profoundly for the better. These people have been around since humans got up off of all fours and started walking on two legs. Quite frankly the first human to do that was living outside the box and it probably created much angst among the rest of the tribe.

Modern American entrepreneurs like Henry Ford, John D. Rockefeller, J. P. Morgan, Dr. Jonas Salk, General George Patton, Steve Jobs, Bill Gates, Larry Ellison, and many others have changed the world in profound, positive ways. All of these people lived outside of the box and accepted no barriers.

It is people like those and to future innovators and dream warriors to whom this book is dedicated. Without such people, as humans we would still be walking around on all fours and foraging for food. Our upward mobility as a species depends on the efforts of these quirky, fearless people driven by ambition and fueled by activity. The big problems of today such as food insecurity, poor communications, poverty, envy, and ignorance will not be solved by people who are comfortable in their box; these problems will be solved by men and women who throw caution to the wind and toss the chains of mental bondage away to dedicate their lives to *Living Outside the Box.*

Living Outside the Box

Living Outside the Box

Chapter One

When the World Was Flat

"When people thought the Earth was flat, they were wrong. When people thought the Earth was spherical, they were wrong. But if you think that thinking the Earth is spherical is just as wrong as thinking the Earth is flat, then your view is wronger than both of them put together."

                                        Isaac Asimov, The Relativity of Wrong

The human race has always looked at the world and the living things on the earth through human-centric eyes. There was a time when it was widely believed that the earth was flat. People believed this because for the most part their lives were lived in very small regions and believing in a flat earth served their purposes just fine. Their towns were small and their farms were within walking distance of the towns where markets were set up so trade could happen. Bartering was widespread and infrastructure had not yet become ubiquitous. Today most people live within forty miles of where they were born but when the earth was believed to be flat most people lived and died without ever traveling more than forty miles from home. For the vast majority of the ancient world, believing in the theory of a flat earth did not cause any day-to-day disruptions.

Living Outside the Box

There were always people who would climb up hills or stand on the shore of the ocean, observing the curve of the earth, yet there was very little reason to question the widespread belief that the earth was flat. Long-range navigation in the desert or in sailing vessels made navigation tools necessary when the distances traveled became so far that the travelers could not find their way home with landmarks or memory. Eventually the stars were identified as useful in determining position, and the algebraic metrics of angles and distances were developed to aid in navigation. Long-range travel was the enlightener to the now accepted fact that the earth is not flat. Finding food sources; seeking gold and other forms of wealth; and waging war necessitated long-distance travel. While experience slowly convinced these early travelers that the world was round, it was not until the 1500s that the globe was successfully circumnavigated. Today a supersonic airplane can circle the earth in a matter of hours and know within a matter of seconds where it is with respect to any geographic point on earth. It took hundreds of years of scientists and explorers living outside of the box of the day with a willingness to risk their lives for this transformational knowledge to be accepted by the rest of humanity. It must be noted that there are still some people who believe that the earth is flat. Their numbers are fortunately fewer than the number who believe that Elvis is alive.

The point of this chapter is that as knowledge is gained, people's perceptions change with that knowledge. It is also to acknowledge that all human beings do not learn things at the same time, nor do they always readily accept advances in knowledge as their new reality. Advancing knowledge requires thinking and living outside the box. Dissemination of newly-found knowledge to the masses takes time, and assumes a capacity to understand the new discoveries. Some widely-held scientific beliefs from the past are now known to be so incorrect that most of them would be the object of comedians.

Flat Earth Medicine

Practicing medicine in the days when the earth was flat put the term practice – in the modern sense of the term – to shame. Each village had a healer who prescribed and administered all sorts of rituals that are currently called protocols. Some of these medical practitioners, like Merlin, the Wizard of King Arthur's Court, were legends, but others were real people. Medical practitioners from prior to the Renaissance were often multi-talented individuals with academic and religious titles to complement their status as healers. In spite of some impactful work in understanding the ways that human bodies react to infection and injury, much of the medicine of those days had its origin in folklore, religion, or other things that today would be considered dangerous and nonsensical.

The Hippocratic Oath that in today's world is thought to bind doctors to a pledge to "first do no harm" did not start out with such a noble admonishment. The original Hippocratic Oath from ancient Greece was crafted more to maintain physicians' loyalty to those who trained them and to the gods of the day.

Living Outside the Box

The first lines of the Hippocratic Oath as translated from the original Greek are as follows:

"I swear by Apollo the physician and Asclepius, and Hygieia and Panacea and all the gods and goddesses as my witnesses, that according to my ability and judgment, I will keep this Oath and this contract:

To hold he who taught me this art equally dear to me as my parent, to be a partner in life with him, and to fulfil his needs when required; to look upon his offspring as equal to my own siblings, and to teach them this art, if they shall wish to learn it, without fee or contract; and that by the set rules, lectures, and every other mode of instruction, I will impart a knowledge of the art to my own sons, and those of my teachers, and to students bound by this contract for having sworn this Oath to the law of medicine but to no others."

The original Hippocratic Oath goes on to pledge to maintain a good diet, to never induce abortions, to be pure in life, to never use a knife unless trained to use it, to never use one's status as a doctor to seduce women or men whether they are free or slaves and to maintain the confidentiality of patients and their ailments.

The interesting thing about the original Hippocratic Oath is that it basically is an oath administered to physicians to forbid them from living outside the box and blazing new trails in medicine. It furthermore restricts the field of medicine to those who are accepted by a teacher (or maybe an emissary from the gods) and their families. If there was ever a document that eliminates the possibility for innovation in a critical field, this is it. It also comes with the implicit endorsement of the gods of the time bringing even more power to the established body of medical practitioners at that time.

As time moved forward, all sorts of cures that have been exposed as frauds such as bloodletting, the touch of members of royal families, the casting of spells, purification by pain, blessings after a sneeze, and curing gout with a poultice of dead owls mixed with other forest remnants.

The now-debunked cures for infections continued for over 3,000 years. Bacteria were first observed in 1676 but antibiotics were not invented until 1928 when Alexander Fleming formulated penicillin. Penicillin launched an age of the development of antibiotics and other antimicrobial therapies: arguably the greatest achievements of modern medicine.

The medical educational establishment of the 1940s much like the ancient Greek practitioners resisted change to innovative treatments as evidenced by a recommendation to prescribe bloodletting to treat pneumonia in William Osler's 1942 text book for medical students called *Principles and Practice of Medicine*. The scientific method of observation, followed by experimentation, then measurement and assessment wasn't used widely until the middle 1600s.

The early scientists like Francis Bacon, Copernicus, Galilei, and eventually Isaac Newton ushered in the new era where science gained favor and respect. Without these people who thought and lived outside of the box we may well still be subject to being diagnosed in need of a good bloodletting or a royal touch to cure what ails us in times of illness. All of these highly impactful people who challenged the status quo with cognitive thinking and scientific experimentation did so at the risk of persecution and even the pain of death. Medical practitioners and powerful religious leaders of the dark ages were staunch supporters of the status quo, and demonstrated little tolerance for those who dared to explore outside of the box.

Flat Earth Astronomy

Mankind has gazed at the heavens in search of answers to our biggest questions for all of recorded history: there are written records of the night sky from as far back as records have been kept. The Incas in South America, the Aztecs in North America, the ancient Chinese and Indians all have somewhat accurate maps of the stars and planets that can be seen by the naked eye. These observations were beneficial when it came to agriculture, navigation, and inventing the protocol that we now refer to as time.

The heavens were always seen to be the home of supernatural beings known as gods and the modern names associated with many heavenly bodies still reflect the names of ancient gods. Mercury, the first planet from the sun, is named for the messenger for the Roman gods. The second planet, Venus, was named for the goddess of beauty and love. Mars, the Roman god of war and the 4th planet is followed by Jupiter, the king of the Roman gods. Saturn, the 6th planet, is the named for the god of the harvest, and is followed by his father, Uranus. The 8th planet, Neptune, is the god of the sea. Pluto, the 9th planet – recently re-classified as a dwarf planet – shares a name with the god of wealth and ruler of mythology's dark underworld.

Earth, our home planet, is not explicitly named after one of the Roman or Greek gods but does have godly origins that emanate from Gaia, the mother of life.

Ancient astronomy was remarkably accurate considering the limited capacity to see into the heavens. Unsurprisingly, given the notoriously anthropocentric nature of humankind, solar system maps from the 4th century BC show the sun and the five other named planets of the time rotating around the Earth. This was called the geocentric model of the solar system. The heliocentric model – with the sun as center of both solar system and universe – was developed by Copernicus some 2,000 years later. While this model is still accepted, images from high-resolution telescopes have demonstrated that while the solar system has a center point, the universe itself does not.

Newspapers around the world print horoscopes and many people faithfully believe that demeanor and personality is determined by the alignment of the stars and planets at the time of birth. In reality, some Leos are outgoing and Pisces are moody just like the star charts predict, but in other cases the opposite is true.

Time and time again, humans show their fascination with powerful external figures like the stars and planets. By thinking and living outside the box, and challenging the geocentric models that were developed 2,400 years ago, Copernicus and

Living Outside the Box

Galilei set the framework for us to map the universe, one advancement in telescopic technology at a time.

For Galileo Galilei, living outside the box eventually caused him to be condemned to living in a box: a dungeon. Despite the fact that scientists had known for centuries that his theory was correct, the Catholic Church held firmly to their belief that the sun rotated around the Earth as an indisputable fact of scripture. The Catholic Church found Galilei guilty of heresy on April 12, 1633, for his assertions that the Earth was not the center of the universe.

Powerful institutions have never yielded their hold on beliefs without a struggle; moving mankind's knowledge forward by challenging authority with outside-the-box thinking and living is often met with entrenched opposition. That said, Galilei is a legend for the ages, while his inquisitors are merely dead.

Flat Earth Creatures & Superstitions

Human beings have always been a very superstitious lot with a propensity to believe in things that have no validation other than feelings. Superstitions are defined as widely held but unjustified beliefs that resemble a sort of supernatural cause-and-effect.

Whether we are reluctant to make big decisions on Friday the 13th or fearful of crossing the path of a black cat, modern life is still full of superstitions that alter the way people think and act. These superstitions are held by people of all ages and walks of life. There are highly educated people who carry their keys on a lucky rabbit's foot keychain and knock on wood to ward off an unwanted consequence. Many a wishbone from a Thanksgiving turkey have caused competitions and anger among family members who act like their next paycheck depends on pulling the correct end of the wishbone. Some even cross their fingers on the other hand to gain just a little bit of luck when pulling it.

Before the age of science we created creatures in our minds that were used to exert control and fear over others. A favorite of mine as a child was when my great-grandmother, who lived to 101 years of age, would scare us with two different imaginary bad guys. One was the bogeyman who would steal children in the night if they weren't tucked tight into their beds. The second was "Potagitem" who was responsible for all missing treats that we were hoping to eat.

Unlike dinosaurs and early humans, there are no fossils or other records of any of these creatures having ever existed. Yet, even today there are people who believe in legendary creatures like the Loch Ness Monster or Bigfoot. Perhaps these monsters of our minds serve to keep us from going into dangerous places or engaging in behavior that could put us into harm's way.

Humans have believed in any number of formidable-yet-nonexistent creatures throughout the course of written history. Some are magnificent beasts such as dragons, krakens, centaurs, unicorns, griffons, jackalopes, and the hounds of hell. Others take on human forms like satyrs, medusa, Minotaur, werewolves, vampires, fairies, mermaids, goblins, hobgoblins and dear old Santa Claus. Finally, there is a class of mythical creatures who represent the afterlife, such as ghosts, demons, kestrels, banshees, and other assorted apparitions.

Very few of these imaginary creatures and mutants of humans were created to inspire us to higher levels of thought or action. Quite the contrary: these mental torments are for the most part meant to keep us in our place. That place of course is as a member of a society that does not challenge authority, does not dare to think outside of the box, and most certainly would never dare to actually live their life outside expected norms of the society that promotes belief in these artifacts of a less sophisticated time.

In the next chapter, the concept of being eternally aware of what is going on in the world is introduced as a learnable habit. With this skill of keen awareness, the learner is forever poised to identify opportunities and needs. These are the gaps which need to be filled by people who are willing to step outside the box of conformity to make something positive happen.

Living Outside the Box

Living Outside the Box

Chapter Two

Eternal Awareness

"Awareness is all about restoring your freedom to choose what you want instead of what your past imposes on you."

Deepak Chopra

Some people seem to have an insatiable curiosity about what is going on around them. Others are content to go with the flow and avoid the exercise of learning what makes their surroundings tick and more importantly what are the opportunities for improvement that are literally right under their noses. The level of curiosity that a person has is directly proportional to the quantity of opportunities to enjoy life to the fullest or identify things around them that are in need of improvement.

Unique ideas and perspectives are the origins of entrepreneurship. When acted upon, these ideas create changes that often have profoundly positive economic or social outcomes. Successful outcomes are those that make human life better: from wealth-creating businesses, to problem-solving solutions, to elegant services, lives are elevated because somebody noticed an opportunity to act.

Ideas and perspectives germinate in the minds of acutely aware individuals during the day-to-day activity of living. By the powers of observation and through a healthy feeling of discontentment with the status quo, curious visionaries identify potential solutions to society's problems. When these visionaries have ambition, drive, and access to capital, sometimes they become entrepreneurs. When their ideas become successful products and services, the entrepreneurs and their communities can accumulate wealth and enhance the quality of life.

Awareness

"Awareness precedes change."

Robin Sharma

Living a day-to-day lifestyle that is characterized by awareness is vital to people who aspire to become game changers. To solve problems and present solutions, you must be aware of the sources of discomfort and have the initiative to ponder how to improve life for everyone. The status quo is the target. Ideas, thoughts, and awareness are the arrows in the quivers of aspiring high-impact people.

Higher consciousness is just as necessary for invention and technical innovation as it is for the initiation of sweeping social change. It all really starts with the acute awareness and recognition of problems which beg for solutions. Other people's problems are a treasure chest of opportunities for aspiring game-changers who have the curiosity and presence of mind to recognize them.

Acknowledgement

Once a problem has been identified, it is important to progress through a contemplation period for the purpose of accepting that the perceived problem is really a problem. When the problem has been substantiated as such, a move from internal thought processes to external dialogues becomes necessary: stakeholders and other people must be convinced that if a solution is implemented, something will change. At the conclusion of this acknowledgement phase, the investigator will not only have found a problem on which to ponder, but will have gotten outside validation of the need for a solution.

Action

When the need for a solution consumes an investigator to the point of decisive action, something magical happens. The quest for a solution has a way of taking on a life of its own and spontaneously attracting a variety of talented people to the cause. In the initial action stage, potential solutions are formulated and vetted through brainstorming or even through using internet-based open innovation forums. Promising solutions are identified and plans are made to design and test the solution set. Unlike a lifestyle of awareness and acknowledgement of a specific problem, the action phase can take on many forms.

Sometimes the post-"eureka moment" action will be a well-written business plan to seek investment capital. Other times the action will result in a working prototype that can be tested prior to deciding what is needed to truly initiate the commercial actualization of the solution. The action phase can become an endless loop of continuous improvement. Every successive improvement of the product or service should be designed to make the solution better and more available to a wider audience of potential customers.

As Andrew Grove, founder of Intel, admonishes us in his book, *Only the Paranoid Survive*; it is only through blowing up the road you just passed over and making your own solutions obsolete that a business can truly stay in front of competition.

Problems are Opportunities

Where are today's opportunities for innovation and entrepreneurship? We can all benefit from innovation in the areas of food, energy, education, healthcare, logistics, government, travel, workforce development, and a multitude of yet-to-be-defined areas. The same was true 10, 50, and 100 years ago. Therefore a better question might be, "Where are we not in need of positive disruptive change?"

With a heightened sense of awareness, every location in the United States and even across the globe offers opportunities for innovators to foster widespread awareness in the areas of local interests or needs. California's Coachella Valley, where I live, offers such opportunities in renewable energy, art, entertainment, lifestyles, and economic diversity: all areas in which commercial success is quite possible. In contrast, the region also has opportunity born of an environmental hazard: the looming ecological threat at the Salton Sea is screaming for problem solvers to stop just talking and live outside the box to implement solutions. The Salton Sea is one of the best examples on earth of the utter failure of words alone in solving a problem. Volumes of publications have covered the extreme negative implications of complacency, yet after roughly 30 years of words from the chattering class, nothing of substance has been done.

Other regions in the world have similar opportunities along with others that are begging for solutions. The jobs that result from the fusion of creativity and engineering will be jobs that identify, solve and implement the solutions to the world's problems. The investors and the innovators who are bold enough to capitalize on big problems are poised to create wealth and prosperity while making life better for the human race.

When a region is seen as an exemplary place to go for innovative solutions to problems, the world will beat a path to their door. Awareness followed by bold actions are the key ingredients to becoming a problem-solving region.

Important Topics

A general sense of awareness is a vital source for understanding what the most pressing problems are. Living your life in a fog of contentment or an uninformed state of aggravation does not lead to the knowledge of what the real opportunities associated with shortcomings may be. Living outside the box necessitates possessing a competent knowledge of what society needs or wants, and is willing to support financially.

Awareness is more than just maintaining a set of up-to-date facts with respect to what is needed or wanted: it also requires an understanding of the entrenched barriers that may have created the need for change in the first place. Barriers will be discussed in more detail later, but they can come from competitors to a new solution, federal or state laws or regulations, existing contracts that exacerbate efforts to slow down innovation, or even delusional claims that are false but widely accepted as ready for prime time use.

Many of the most challenging needs do not yet have a technically feasible solution. Examples of needs without solutions today are things like transparent materials with the strength of metals and the thermal characteristics of insulation. Entrepreneurs are continually having ideas that have not yet been proven to be technically feasible. Some of these ideas are capable of being proven feasible and others are not. It is important to note that proving a concept does not constitute proof of market. This is frustrating for many entrepreneurs who do have a decent sense of awareness.

Living Outside the Box

There are needs and wants that do have a proven solution that are not (or are not yet) financially feasible in the markets. A recent example that has gone from a novelty item with niche markets at a prohibitive price to a fully feasible consumer power source in a span of less than 20 years is rooftop PV (photovoltaic) solar. Used to generate energy for residential homes, PV solar technology has gone from a very expensive and inefficient energy generation option to a cost effective, easy-to-understand source for self-generated electricity. This all happened in roughly one decade. The payback period for an investment in PV solar is now between 4 and 5 years in regions like Southern California. That corresponds to a 20% to 25% return on cash invested. This certainly passes the threshold test of a good investment.

Twenty years ago the return on investment for PV solar at the residential level was so low that the technology would never pay for itself, and was only the choice for wealthy individuals who wanted to be early adopters without concern for costs.

PV solar is a most cost-effective solution in areas with abundant sun and high energy costs: in areas with electricity costs that are less than 10 cents per kilowatt hour and abundant cloud cover, the cost of installing PV solar is not be justified on a purely financial basis. A push in research and development efforts to increase panel efficiencies is expected to remedy this problem in the next decade. PV solar is a near perfect example of science and government both taking positively impactful actions that have hastened the quality and efficacy of the technology. Moving the PV solar technology forward was a rare example of government, banking, and product development living outside the box to make this a product offering that became desirable to residential customers. It has also played a big part in reducing the United States' emissions of CO_2 and greenhouse gasses into the atmosphere by a world-leading 14% between the years 2000 and 2017.

These examples make it clear that developing a sense of awareness on a high enough level to identify problems, formulate solutions, and make sufficient connections to implement those solutions is no small task. This takes keeping your fingers on the pulse of human discomfort, understanding the barriers to implementation, and continually staying informed of the current state of science. It also takes an inherent understanding of consumer psychology, and a temperament that is willing to embrace and promote disruptive change.

Living Outside the Box

True awareness requires maintaining a current base of knowledge with respect to energy; cybersecurity; politics at federal, state, and local levels; health; science; education; critical infrastructure; product availability; and the projections being made by scholarly analysts for the future. This is a huge, time-consuming exercise that never ends, but it does keep your mind young and engaged. I would suggest that maintaining a sense of heightened awareness is key to keeping yourself both stimulated and relevant. Awareness will make your life better and more enjoyable.

Awareness Techniques

As has long been the case, the best way to maintain awareness of what is going on is by reading. Reading a complement of newspapers – starting with one's local newspaper and followed by national newspapers – will keep the subject matter that is of concern to people in the front of your mind. Two American-based newspapers that address current events in an accurate and timely manner are the Wall Street Journal and the New York Times. Each state has newspapers that are competent with statewide news coverage, such as California's Los Angeles Times and the San Francisco Chronicle. If one's key area of interest is technology, the San Jose Mercury News is a good source to follow.

Nearly all relevant newspapers are available online and are very affordable. For an international perspective, the Economist, Guardian and The Financial Times can be valuable to validate the needs of industrialized nations.

Living Outside the Box

National content aggregators such as the Real Clear publications are another good way to start the day for people who want to maintain awareness. Real Clear aggregates topical issues on a number of subjects that include politics, policy, markets, world, defense, cyber, energy, health, science, religion, education, sports, history, investigations, and life. The website for Real Clear is always followed by the category of interest. For example if one's category of interest is energy the website is www.realclearenergy.com. The other categories work the same way. This particular website posts links to articles that address the issues from both right and left perspectives in politics and is very close to being politically benign in non-political categories.

There are many daily emails that offer unique perspectives on current topics. The best ones that I have found are put out by university-based think tanks such as Stanford University's Hoover Institute which features seasoned thinkers on most timely subjects. While several options are presented here, I encourage diligence in seeking out new and different information sources.

Social media sites such as Facebook have grown as a source for news. The complication of seeking news from social media is the high probability that the users of these sites are not particularly interested in vetting what they post. Many people who post are pushing their own agendas with little regard for accuracy. Social media can be entertaining, and is great for socializing, but has not cleared the bar to become a trusted source for news.

Living Outside the Box

Face-to-face interactions with other humans is still a preferred way to gain information and to test your thoughts out on others. Local chambers of commerce offer opportunities to mingle with the business people of your locale. Gatherings like these are good places to meet connectors and learn about the retail and service businesses that are new to a region.

Keeping up with local government is vital to gaining the knowledge needed to implement solutions in your location of interest. By attending or watching city council meetings and reading their agendas, the opportunity to meet and get to know your elected leaders is an activity that can pay off with friendships and an understanding of the perspective through which legislators make decisions. They are surprisingly easy to approach and get to know, especially if they see you as a problem solver.

State and national elected officials are less available but will typically respond to letters. Government is seen as an impediment to change but in reality that is not always the case. This is especially true before progress-blunting laws are put into place. Political leaders can be vital to gaining support for the implementation of transformational solutions.

Awareness is the first habit to develop in order to become a high impact problem solver. Living outside the box is necessary to effect change, but making connections and knowing who may help or hinder those efforts is also vital. A 5-year project can become a 1-year project when the right connections can agree on an action to be taken.

Living Outside the Box

Heightened awareness can improve life by making one's mind more nimble and responsive, but in addition to these positives, you may also be more attuned to the weaknesses and deficiencies in surrounding systems. In the next chapter I address a most uncomfortable technique that is sometimes necessary to effect positive change: the deliberate willingness to call out the shortcomings in a way that gets sufficient attention to merit action. There is a children's story in which a ruler was fawned over by adults and sycophants for his snazzy dress was really naked. Of course it took an innocent child without any fear of reprisal to point out the reality: the king was naked.

Living Outside the Box

Living Outside the Box

Chapter 3

Exposing Shortcomings: The King is Naked

"Wisdom tends to grow in proportion to one's awareness of one's ignorance."

Anthony de Mello

From a psychological perspective, it is always difficult to go against the flow or to be the lone supporter or opponent of a project or idea. This explains why it is so difficult to call attention to a shortcoming that others have defined as adequate. For most human beings, change is something to avoid; for those who have what it takes to live outside the box, change is a necessary activity. Those who resist change will often simply deny the need for it. This can happen for myriad reasons: protecting a job; protecting someone else's job; or protecting the gravy train of a powerful and perhaps less-than-necessary cabal.

Well-meaning change agents have always run headlong into the resistance of powerful people with financial interests in maintaining the status quo, even when the status quo is suboptimal. Often, when the financial interests of an individual or group are dependent on the status quo, the situation in question is at least nefarious and often should be illegal. It should be noted that whistleblowing on illegal activities is beyond the scope of this book: it can be a dangerous undertaking and guidance on the subject should be left to law enforcement authorities.

Living Outside the Box

The children's book *The Emperor's New Clothes*, is a classic
example, written to teach children about such situations.
Written by Hans Christian Andersen, the tale tells of a pair of
weavers who convince the vain emperor that they will make him
a new suit of clothes that is invisible to those who are unfit for
their positions, stupid, or incompetent. In reality, they make no
clothes at all, and even succeed in making all of the emperor's
subjects believe the clothes are invisible to them. This ends with
the emperor strutting around town while indulging his
superiority complex before his inferior subjects. Of course the
townspeople accepted the ruse that they were nothing but a
bunch of less-than-worthy country bumpkins, and so praised the
emperor for the elegant new suit he was wearing. To behave
differently and face reality that the emperor was parading
around naked would have amounted to a confirmation of their
own stupidity. The weavers' ruse was finally exposed when a
child believed his own eyes and blurted out, "the emperor is not
wearing any clothes!" At this, the townspeople realized that they
had been had and laughed at the naked emperor. The emperor,
who had bought into the ruse, continued his parade, but
eventually reality set in and the emperor realized that he had
been the victim of a fraud. Of course, the weavers had left the
region with a good portion of the emperor's gold in their
pockets.

As a child, I often wondered why it took a child to blurt out the
truth that the emperor was naked. What could possibly make an
entire town of adults defy what they saw and actually
compliment the emperor for clothes he was not wearing? I

would submit that the driving factor was fear. Fear of losing one's job, fear of being thought to be a fool, fear of not being a part of the crowd, and even fear of retribution from a person of power is what drove the adults in the story. In contrast, the child had nothing to lose, and did not fear calling the naked emperor out for his own foolish pride.

Realities like this play out in everyday life all over the United States and the world. There are bosses who are clueless about what is needed for their businesses who are fawned over by their staffs, even when they are fully aware that "the boss is not competent." There are elected officials at all levels of government that have no idea what their communities, states, or even countries need to make life better. Some are driven by ego and superiority complexes that would make the emperor in the previous story blush. In spite of this most people are quite reluctant to point out the shortcomings of elected officials because of the power that they have over contracts, law enforcement and the media. Afraid of the whisper campaigns that can be waged against them by powerful yet incompetent people, many people make the conscious decision to remain quiet and let the incompetence continue. Eventually someone usually comes along who has the courage to live outside the box and expose the incompetence, and it doesn't take long for most of the quiet enablers get on board quickly.

Being willing to expose shortcomings is not the same thing as being a whistleblower who exposes criminal activity and often collects a bounty for doing so. While they are definitely living outside the box, whistleblowers have a special kind of courage. Ultimately they have the law on their side and as long as we have the rule of law, whistleblowers will have some semblance of protection.

The act of exposing shortcomings is often one that does not really have any opposition. In some cases it simply challenges the status quo in a way that calls for new solutions and change. In other cases there are intrinsic reasons that change is required.

Every significant technological achievement faces resistance and reluctance when it comes to adoption. Before electric lights, many big cities had gas lighting that literally were open flames in public places to provide light. Small communities at that time had no public lighting at all.

When electric lights were first considered there was fear, resistance, and ignorance poised to stop it. On December 26, in 1878, John Wanamaker, brought electric lighting to his store in Philadelphia, the first ever department store to do so. This adoption of new lighting technology met resistance from customers and outsiders alike. A year later Wannamaker's became the first department store to have telephones. Wannamaker also pioneered the practice of allowing customers to return merchandise. John Wannamaker was an early retailer in the United States who was an early adopter of technology and a man who lived outside the box in setting an example for other large elegant retailers like Macy's, Bloomingdale's, and J. C. Penney.

Living Outside the Box

With every major advance that involved large disruptions to the status quo, it has taken someone who had a vision and a willingness to live outside the box to move things forward. Horseless carriages – that we now refer to as automobiles – had massive resistance from people who had a financial interest in keeping us on horses. Radio and television were both looked on with reluctance from people who were fearful of direct communication with the masses and even from religious organizations. In the early stage of the computer industry, when higher mathematics was dependent on students mastering the use of slide rules (my high school years) much resistance was directed toward the $300 calculators that Hewlett Packard and Texas Instruments offered that really were only capable of basic arithmetic. After all, if students had calculators they would lose their ability to do math. When compact discs were introduced there was resistance from the record industry. When digital music distribution was enabled by the internet, compact disc makers resisted. Similarly, traditional movie theatres are now concerned that Netflix will be their Waterloo and some have resisted, even though data refutes this for now.

In a local example, my speech at the 2017 CVEP Economic Summit pointed out that the Coachella Valley was at a disadvantage to other regions because the bandwidth offered is not sufficient to upload large files in a timely manner. The example that really got the point across was when our audience was asked if they had ever had a Netflix movie crash and default to a spinning circle on the screen. The room was full of 600 civic and business leaders, and they all got the point immediately. To recognize that the spinning circle was a bandwidth issue took awareness and knowledge. To point out to a room full of leaders who did not know this was a deliberate decision to live outside the box with the desire that it would inspire the audience to do the same. I made this choice knowing fully that there were influential people in the room with a financial interest in maintaining the appearance that all is well and good. By 2018 the bandwidth in the region had doubled and it seems to be common accepted knowledge that bandwidth is in need of improvement. Bandwidth is one of those things that needs continuous improvement and thus far the lesson seems to have been well received.

My assertions met no real resistance with the exceptions of the bandwidth providers who were not ready to admit that their product was in desperate need of being upgraded. I am now optimistic that this will work out over time and there has been one profoundly positive step forward with respect to providing ultra-high bandwidth to start-up companies. This deal-making innovation will be visited further in Chapter 9.

Exposing shortcomings is something that does not come without personal risk. That being the case, it is best to pick the battles that can be won with the help of others. Success has a thousand parents: it is quite fulfilling to gain the respect of other people for being willing to come to the defense of the region you call home and expose things that need change that can be changed. There is no shortcoming too small or too large to be exposed if your techniques for exposing it are in the public's best interest.

For the record, the three things that my speech called out as needing improvement in 2017 were bandwidth, local investment, and a full service destination public university that offers STEM (science, technology, engineering, and math) degrees. These are all things that we have influence over but no ability to execute without the resources and actions of other local and regional leaders. Since that time, much progress has been made in two of the first two areas but local investment in home-grown entrepreneurs remains elusive.

In my speech at the 2018 economic summit, I added two more things to the list, along with a third opportunity, showcasing them in a four-minute video. One of these was widely known and has been documented for several decades: the looming environmental disaster at the Salton Sea. For years, various government entities have publically claimed responsibility for solving this problem; the 2018 video intentionally turned the complacency of these agencies into an opportunity. If real efforts and actions replace the empty words of the past two decades, the visual depiction of the north shore of the Salton Sea could become a reality by 2050.

A second opportunity for the Eastern Coachella Valley was also embedded into the video. An inter-modal facility headquartered at the Jackie Cochran airport, an older airfield that has been utilized for private aviation but not for rail or highway trade, was called for.

Living Outside the Box

Perpetual awareness, a willingness to live outside the box, and having the courage to call out shortcomings are the foundations for forming a vision, which is the subject of the next chapter.

"Faced with the choice between changing one's mind and proving that there is no need to do so, almost everybody gets busy on the proof"

John Kenneth Galbraith

Living Outside the Box

Living Outside the Box

Chapter 4

Developing and Maintaining a Vision

"Vision without action is merely a dream. Action without vision just passes the time. Vision with action can change the world."

Joel A. Barker

Throughout human history, there has been a persistent need for people who could develop a vision. From young children who close their eyes, imagining themselves standing on a platform to receive an honor, to an elderly person who struggles to gain acceptance for an idea hatched long ago, visioning is the crucible of progress. As an exercise, visioning is fulfilling, and provides instant feedback, either internally or from peers. Without vision, there is no call to action, yet a vision without actions to put it into motion is nothing but a delusional mental exercise.

Participating in a visioning exercise can be frustrating; when a visioning exercise starts out with no focus, many times absolutely nothing comes from it. Cities across the United States have often attempted to engage their citizens in what they call visioning to try to get input on what ideas might be out there to solve nagging problems. One common municipal visioning exercise is to call a hundred or so citizens together to discuss what can be done to jumpstart a downtown that is a couple of decades past its expiration date. Having participated in several such exercises, I can say that these kinds of sessions are not

52

always really seeking citizen input. The facilitation is often done by groups that are puppet organizations for entrenched protectors of the status quo. In the worst examples, the facilitators can be seeded with ideas from the protectors of the status quo that will serve to enhance their wealth and/or power.

Avoiding False Visions

Across the country, cities large and small have had periods of infatuation with the siren song of how economically impactful sports and entertainment venues claim to be. City after city has borrowed money to build a downtown temple to sports, only to learn after a few years that the projections of financial returns were only concocted to get them to spend massive sums of money on construction projects. In other cases, rather than building and operating stadiums, cities have provided subsidies to team owners under the assumption that economic prosperity will follow games. While most are only paltry sums in the hundreds of millions, some of these subsidies have reached over a billion dollars.

There are numerous after-the-fact analyses that refute the claims made by those who want to generate economic impact by subsidizing stadiums. One particular study by Dennis Coats of the Mercatus Center at George Mason University actually concluded empirically after 15 years that per capita income of the surrounding region decreased:

Living Outside the Box

To be very clear: the conclusion is that one of the most important metrics of any local economy, per capita income, is diminished after a stadium is subsidized. That means things got worse after the stadium was built. Even with over two decades of studies showing conclusive negative returns, the vision of stimulating an economy with a stadium is alive and well in local governments. Of course the stadium-building contractors are ready and willing to return the favor in the form of campaign contributions to line the coffers of the elected officials who handed them the lucrative contracts.

Dennis Coats, Mercatus Center, George Mason University

...the entire sports environment matters for the level of real personal income per capita, in the sense that the array of sports variables are jointly statistically significant. But contrary to the promised increase, the presence of a major sports franchise lowers the income.

Subsidy advocates often make claims about job creation when advocating for big stadium projects. In one case, in downtown Evansville, Indiana, the proponents actually claimed that replacing a 12,000 seat stadium that supported several hundred jobs with a 10,000 seat stadium that supported the same jobs somehow constituted creation of those several hundred jobs.

Living Outside the Box

Many educated people took the bait and took up the banner that moving jobs was the same as creating jobs. After seven years the shiny new downtown arena is not paying for its debt to be serviced, and has never achieved positive operating cash flow.

The downtown Evansville stadium (Ford Center) has consumed roughly $9 million taxpayer dollars per year that could have been used for other purposes. At this point the un-projected cash flow shortages from operating and servicing the debt for the Ford Center have passed the $50 million mark with no path to positive cash flow.

Critical infrastructure like the sewers, roads, sidewalks, and antiquated water pipes are still in a state of decay and the modernization will eventually cost in excess of a billion dollars.

This was a case of misplaced vision of the few at the expense of the many. This is a trap to be avoided in the visioning process.

Keep the Vision Broad and Positive

Visions that positively impact many people while elevating the local economy are worthy of discussion and exploration without bounds. In the case of economic development across the country, the mission drives the visioning process, and the visioning process is never complete. A broad vision that will take a number of years to realize, but the positive impacts begin early in the process and magnify as time goes forward. The annual budget for owning these efforts is also a small fraction of what the interest on the bonds floated for a big capital project like a sports stadium would be.

Living Outside the Box

Visions did not happen overnight or come from a series of community meetings. Impactful visions happened organically over a number of years during which economic development leaders and their staffs operate in a heightened state of awareness about what their region has, what is desired, and what actions will put the region on a path to elevate the economy in a

CVEP's Mission

The mission is to diversify the economy of the Coachella Valley by growing those non-cyclical business sectors that pay a "thriving" wage as opposed to the often-called-for "living" wage.

non-cyclical yet sustainable way.

The Beginning of the Coachella Valley's Vision

Using the mission as a starting point, in 2011 some insightful public officials set one of the fundamental visions into motion. That was to deliberately take actions to foster entrepreneurship in technical business sectors, focusing on those sectors which had the basic building blocks in place to use as a launch platform. The chosen area of specialization was renewable energy. The Coachella Valley is bounded on the west by the San Gorgonio Pass, which is a natural wind tunnel through which the cool moist air of the Pacific Ocean makes its way to the desert. This micro-climate zone is home to roughly 4,000 commercial wind turbines that are often in need of upgrading

56

and maintenance. The region is also one of the best places on earth to catch the sun's energy and convert it into electricity, making us a cost effective place for ramping up residential and commercial solar energy. The south end of the Salton Sea is also one of the world's best places to harvest geothermal energy from the earth. This combination of multiple natural resources in a small region makes the Coachella Valley an unrivaled location to realize the benefits of renewable energy.

The need to stabilize the electrical grid and the nagging fact that the sun sets at night made the next logical step to include energy management and battery storage as targeted technologies.

The initial vision of fostering entrepreneurship was actualized with the establishment of the Palm Springs iHub. This vision was later further advanced by opening Palm Springs Accelerator Campus as a home for companies that have proven their concepts and are ready to manufacture.

After seven years the Palm Springs iHub has accepted over 70 start-up technology companies into the program and is regarded by the State of California's Office of Business and Economic Development as the most impactful and best-managed of the 16 California Innovation Hubs.

CVEP Awards 2014 - 2019

Spirit of the Entrepreneur: CSU San Bernardino

*Clean Air Award: South Coast Air Quality
Management District*

SBEMP Outstanding Leadership

Martin Luther King Legacy of Service Award

LifeStream Humanitarian of the Year

The Palm Springs iHub and CVEP have also received numerous commendations from the California Assembly and Senate for the achievements of the first seven years in operation. Rather than resting on these laurels and confining our efforts to keeping the good activities going forward, we are embarking on a new series of activities to leverage the accomplishments of our early years to elevate even further.

In 2019, another iHub in Palm Desert that will specialize in digital technology such as cybersecurity, the internet of things (IoT), and 5G communications. These choices and decisions came about as a direct result of the successes of the past and the awareness of the present which will be addressed in the next segment.

Expanding on the Vision

A vision in motion is a vision with momentum. The momentum gained with the operation of the Palm Springs iHub created a buzz around fostering entrepreneurship in the greater Palm Springs region. In 2018 the City of Palm Desert City Council voted unanimously to establish a digital iHub in Palm Desert and to contract with CVEP to be the operator. This decision was not taken lightly and considered some of the opportunities for valley-wide improvement that were identified during the period from 2015 to 2018 when the focus on entrepreneurial impact was heightened.

At the 2017 CVEP Economic Summit, my presentation included a call for three critical things that were needed to accelerate the potential impact of entrepreneurship on the Coachella Valley. The first and most important was identified as a comprehensive destination university that offers STEM degrees. The second was state-of-the-art bandwidth, and the third was significant local equity investment in the start-up companies accepted into the iHub program. The leadership of the region has substantially accepted these three "shortcomings" as things that need to be addressed over time. The importance of these three needs cannot be overemphasized.

Currently the Coachella Valley is served by the College of the Desert (COD), a classic community college with all of the programs that community colleges typically offer at a very affordable price. Students at COD who complete their programs can expect to leave the campus with a valuable skill that elevates their value and/or two years of traditional education that has prepared them for a four-year university and beyond.

The Coachella Valley at this time does not have a public four-year university that offers a full complement of degrees, meaning no four-year STEM degrees are available. This situation presents a need that can only be addressed by expanding the current California State University at San Bernardino Palm Desert Campus to offer STEM degrees. Technology companies are reluctant to locate – and have challenges growing – anywhere that STEM degrees are not offered. Being the advocate of the expansion of CSUSB-PDC into a comprehensive stand-alone campus is now a part of the vision to address our mission.

In chapter 3, I shared how the region's bandwidth needs were taught to community leaders using the example of Netflix interruptions, which reached attendees on a personal level. Bandwidth is a game-changer in digital businesses, even outside of the entertainment business. This was learned the hard way when our GIS (geographic information systems) director attempted to upload some data and image-intensive files to a client business that was located 60 miles away. Due to slow upload speeds, the upload took six hours. An alternative would have been to burn the files onto a CD ROM and drive it to the client. By the time the upload of the file got there, you could have driven the disk to the client, driven home, eaten dinner and watched a movie on Netflix.

Imagine if the files had been medical images, urgently sent for the opinion of a respected surgeon in another location. Telemedicine and second opinions from afar are dependent on a level of bandwidth that was not available; sufficient bandwidth to have transferred the file did not exist at the time. Thus the vision to advocate for increasing the bandwidth available in the Greater Palm Springs region has been adopted. It is vital to digital businesses to flourish, and in many ways it is just as important as a comprehensive university.

The final "shortcoming" that was pointed out at the 2017 Economic Summit is the need for local investment capital. This is a lesser need than bandwidth, but is nevertheless vital for financial reasons. The obvious reason for local investment is so that the gains in the stock prices in iHub companies are accretive to the local residents. The United States is full of factories that are owned by foreign corporations that do indeed create hundreds of thousands of jobs for our citizens. The "shortcoming" with that business model is that the profits and equity appreciation are repatriated to the owners, who do not live here.

The iHub companies to date have raised roughly $30 million in equity financing. Less than one million of those dollars were sourced locally. The region is essentially missing out on the appreciation associated with profit growth, liquidity events, and those dollars are going elsewhere. The iHub companies have shown that people or firms from other locations are willing to invest in proven intellectual property. It would be better for the region if the investments were made locally.

The Broad Benefits of Vision

Benefits of CVEP's Vision

Increased per capita earnings

Improved educational attainment

Higher-skilled workforce

Higher aspirations among young people

Insulation against automation's impacts on employment

Enhanced entrepreneurial activity

Establishment of equity investment opportunities

Decreased dependence on cyclical businesses

Elevate the overall quality of life

Raise the tax base

These are the kinds of things that drive significant regional transformation and substantially benefit the entire population and are therefore worthy of focus and efforts.

In the next chapter the exercise of recognizing things that have high levels of potential and how to connect people in purposeful ways will be addressed. Forming a vision with wide positive impact is difficult. Getting community leaders and investors to stay the course to realize the potential is even more difficult, but imminently achievable and always worth the effort.

"A vision is not just a picture of what could be; it is an appeal to our better selves, a call to become something more."

Rosabeth Moss Kanter

Living Outside the Box

Living Outside the Box

Chapter 5

Recognizing and Connecting the Dots

"It's not about what it is, it's about what it can become."

Dr. Seuss

Perhaps one of the most referred-to clichés among the gathering class is the one about how important it is to be able to connect the dots. While connections are a very important activity when it comes to team- building and awareness, without the knowledge of what you need to connect, these gatherings are of little consequence when it comes to innovation or problem solving. The inconvenient reality about people who only talk about connecting the dots is that many of them wouldn't be able to recognize a "dot" if it was served to them alongside their dinner.

In this context, dots refer to things of potential significance. Going back to the earlier example of the invention of the chariot, the things of potential significance (the dots) were the wheel and the box. It took 300 years of making pottery on wheels, and storing pottery along with other items of value in boxes, for someone to connect the two as a potential facilitator of transportation. Attaching the wheels to the box in a way that did not restrict rotation was the breakthrough. Whomever did that became the inventor of the axle before intellectual property was protected or even considered valuable. Voila! At that moment some ancient form of a little red wagon was invented.

Living Outside the Box

The original handle was in all likelihood the human arm but after a decade of splinters and callouses the handle was added to the miracle of the wheel-and-box combination. The iterations continued, and eventually the wheels and box were strong enough to hold a human, and a horse was added. Since that day some 3,200 years ago we have had rolling boxes that transport us from one place to another. Without that early exercise of recognizing the dots and connecting them, we may still be walking from one place to another.

Recognizing dots requires many different habits and abilities. It does leverage awareness of things that are available but it also draws on the ability to hold seemingly insignificant objects in our memories along with things of potential significance until the next embodiment comes along in the form of an idea. Heightened awareness coupled with memory puts you in a position to connect the dots. In the business incubation industry, the willingness to live outside the box by doing more than just talking about these connections is the path to what we refer to as proof of concept. Proof of concept is the first step in the product development cycle: the foundation for tangible progress in both tangible and intangible business models.

Recognizing significant things is seeing the added potential and value that these things may have when used in novel ways and/or combinations. Sometimes it takes exposure to other people in order to see where innovations might fit in the grand scheme of things. You can learn the habits that enable the recognition of significant things with great potential. Bringing about positive impacts often takes casual conversations with other people of various backgrounds and professions to identify ways to inspire new embodiments of these significant things. Following is series of descriptions of some of the dots that are ready to be connected in a myriad of ways.

Distributed Production

Distributed production is a long-standing practice, but it didn't get a name until difficulties arose after the broad implementation of centralized planning and production. Centralization is defined as a system that places all authority under the control of a single organization. Centralization typically results in having critical production facilities large distances away from the customers.

One of the most nagging difficulties associated with centralized production are the problems associated with distribution. This is a double edged sword with the supply chain and the distribution logistics. Furthermore the needs of the customer base are lost across the distances and minimized by the monopolistic nature of centralization.

Let's use the example of bats for youth baseball and softball players. The target customers are little-league-aged children, between the ages of 9 and 12, who like to play baseball or softball. In a purely centralized production system, all bats would be made in one location. This presents a set of problems since baseball and softball are played in nearly every country. Until the last decade, most bats were manufactured in a handful of factories and had to be shipped to customers. To get a

Living Outside the Box

Louisville Slugger bat from a factory in Louisville, Kentucky into the hands of a 12-year-old in rural New Mexico involved transactions between the bat factory and a distributor; a distributor and a retailer; multiple channels of transportation; and finally a transaction between a retail establishment and a 12-year-old child. All of this handling and shipping is cumbersome and expensive. It also sets up a classic situation in which the 12-year-old almost never gets the optimal bat for their personal use.

Centralized production has created logjams and delays in industries from car parts to food-making ingredients. The term "waiting for parts" has been woven into our way of life for more than a century. While there are benefits associated with centralized production when it comes to repeatability and efficiency, the trade-off is customer satisfaction and inefficiency in distribution.

Living Outside the Box

There are already services that will take measurements for custom clothing remotely and transmit the data to a location where the clothing is made for rapid shipment to the customer. There is no reason that at some point in the future the 12-year-old in the previous example could not be measured for a bat that is optimized to his or her strength and size. The data could then be transmitted to a local 3-D production center and in a matter of hours the young person could receive the perfectly fitted new bat. In this case, the distribution and retail steps are essentially eliminated and the customer is ultimately served better than before.

Centralized Planning and the USSR

Centralized planning was the stake through the heart of the former Soviet Union. They were many years behind the capitalistic western nations in nearly everything. The USSR (Union of Soviet Socialist Republics) was behind the west in offering shoes that were made for right and left feet, and even in getting potatoes from the farm to the cities. Eventually that system of governance and commerce failed and the USSR split into many countries.

Distributed production happens when the production happens as close to the point of use as possible. Farmers' markets come fairly close to simulating distributed production when food grown locally is made available in a public location for local people to buy and prepare. Farmers' markets were the norm for centuries until centralized operations created megastores. Recently in food production there has been a return to farmers' markets and even to backyard chicken farming in municipalities that allow such activities.

Perhaps the most familiar embodiment of distributed production that is rapidly expanding is in rooftop generation of electricity. The most widely adopted technology used to generate electricity at the individual level is PV (photovoltaic) solar panels. PV solar panels were "dots" a decade ago, but the dots have been connected with racking, inverter technology, smart meters, willing financiers, and legislation to make this solution – for the most part – available to all.

With PV solar, the aforementioned combination of solar panels, wires, inverters, meters, and contracts enable a customer to generate the electricity that is used in his or her own home right on their own rooftop. The amortized cost to generate this power ranges from 4 to 16 cents per kilowatt hour, depending on variables that include geographic location and weather. This cost structure is competitive with prices offered by public utilities in many parts of the United States and is expected to be competitive everywhere in the near future.

In California those who generate power on their rooftops are credited for that production directly by the electricity providers up to the limit of their personal use. The credits even extend into the evening so that overproduction during the day time can be used to cover evening use. With a properly sized system one can produce all of the power needed during the day to provide electricity at night without having any battery storage. In California, at least, smart meters plus friendly legislation combine to work like a free battery.

There are even provisions to be compensated for overproduction but the rate is at the utility's average wholesale rate, which is roughly 6 cents per kilowatt hour. The utility then sells that power at the rates approved by the California Utilities Commission: from 13 to 36 cents per kilowatt hour. The public utilities also limit the number of solar panels through a contract known as a power purchase agreement, so as citizen generators you can't really compete with them in a significant way.

It would be welcome to be able to maximize rooftop electrical generation and sell it to our friends and neighbors at or near public utility pricing. The technology to do so currently exists but the dots are not connected to enable this to happen. Later in this chapter we will show an example of how to connect the dots to make this happen in a way that makes every rooftop a cash generation engine that may well threaten the business model of centralized power generation.

As a reminder, the "dot" in this case is distributed production. Through distributed production, the losses typically associated with transportation and distribution are eliminated. By dispersing production assets, businesses will realize a reduced sensitivity to disruption of centralized operations from natural disasters, errors of judgment, failure of elements, or political disruptions. Distributed production is the way of the future: from food and energy production to data storage and management and most points in between. It is one of the enabling thought processes for successfully living outside the box and changing existing things for the better.

Blockchain

In <u>*The Blockchain Revolution*</u>, authors Don and Alex Tapscott describe blockchain technology as "an incorruptible digital ledger of economic transactions that can be programmed to record not just financial transactions but virtually everything of value." In a world where everything from news to food safety to election results have been alleged to have been tampered with, an incorruptible ledger of any sort will provide both security and value to trade and transactions of all types. The use of blockchain technology in areas where trust has been diminished or never established could literally improve our belief systems, from governance to the kitchen table.

Blockchain is still in the development stage for most applications. The most advanced application for blockchain has been for transactions involving crypto currencies. Crypto currencies are another "dot" that garnered much attention during 2018 for wide swings in value but we will not address crypto in this book. I will illustrate why blockchain has the potential to be a world-changer, and will close with a scenario that may someday enable us all to be electricity providers if we so choose.

Blockchain, in its highest embodiment, has the potential to become to data what rooftop solar has become to electricity generation. Imagine that you could lease out unutilized data storage capacity on a laptop, desktop, or even a personal server to whoever was willing to pay for it. Imagine further that you would be able to feel secure in transactions with people you have never met, and feel secure with them utilizing the extra storage on your electronic devices. That may seem far-fetched, but services like Airbnb and VRBO make this kind of transaction possible for surplus space in homes. Those are examples of distributed production of lodging. Uber and Lyft have done the same with ground transportation: making rides securely available in the personal vehicles of strangers who are selling their surplus availability one ride at a time. This is distributed transportation.

The trend is moving toward distributing all production and services as close as possible to consumption. Blockchain technology is becoming the preferred consideration for removing risks and assuring fidelity in enabling these types of transactions.

By allowing documents, contracts, or states of being to be stored identically across a number of computers and using encryption to assure that no changes are made after entry, blockchain is foundational to bringing trust and security to the curation process. Blockchain is the tool for real time audits of all processes. Today if one wants to share a document it is does so by first sharing a file. Then the person that the file is shared with can make changes and send them back to the original sender. The document gets completed when the two or more people have all serially completed their changes and agreed upon the final version. This is a time consuming process that is ripe for errors. In a blockchain-enabled process a file can be placed on the blockchain by the originator which makes the file available to everyone who has access to the blockchain. The original file is encrypted so it is preserved in its original state in perpetuity. The other members of the blockchain can now access the file and create new versions simultaneously, with each iteration being preserved and encrypted again. Encryption in a blockchain is called a "hash," and these hashes are the key to data integrity.

Just as driving a car does not require knowledge of how the internal combustion engine works and using a computer does not require a user to understand microprocessors and gate arrays, one does not need to understand blockchain technology to use it. When a blockchain is put into place using it will be as easy as learning how to drive or use a spreadsheet. This means that rapid adoption will be ubiquitous, as with other distributed activities like rooftop generation of electricity.

Blockchain + Rooftop Solar = Personal Power Plants

Imagine the previously discussed opportunity to generate as much rooftop power as possible and to sell it to friends, neighborhoods, and strangers on your block at market rates. By creating a blockchain to provide a ledger of electricity production and combining that with the means to account for the use of power by a nearby residence, expanding or establishing solar rooftops to exceed personal use becomes an investment decision. For instance, if one's rooftop can be configured to produce 16,000 kilowatt hours more than the home uses, and the excess can be sold at market rates, that rooftop can become a profit center or an extra retirement check. In California if that overproduction could be sold at market rates in the daytime, the 16,000 kilowatt hours will generate an annual income of between $2,500 and $5,000 depending on location. With an installation cost of roughly $25,000, the homeowner would realize an annualized return on investment of between 10% and 20%, which significantly exceeds current returns offered by banks.

Relatively expensive electricity and ample sunshine make the financial case for turning your rooftop into a profit center an easy one in Southern California. By combining blockchain technology and rooftop solar, not only is a high return on investment made available to investors, but the clean energy generated will reduce CO_2 and greenhouse gas emissions, making the world a better and more sustainable place. The only barriers to implementing this are homeowner-friendly legislation and trust by neighbors that the energy provided is of sufficient quality to be safe and useable.

Growing up in rural Kentucky, our family and three others worked together every summer to grow a large garden. Our next door neighbor provided a plot of land of sufficient size and the rest of the families provided the seeds, seedlings, and fertilizer. We all shared in the labor of weeding and picking and no one kept track of time. We had fresh corn, green beans, radishes, potatoes, squash, tomatoes, zucchinis, and occasionally watermelons and cantaloupes. Excess vegetables were canned for winter. We did not have a blockchain but we did have trust. Blockchain technology can and most certainly will make such things possible by providing a third party ledger of trust to all transactions that adopt it.

In addition to the enabling of sharing economy models, blockchain is being implemented to assist with contract development, peer to peer markets, governance, supply chain auditing, file storage, predictive marketing, protection of intellectual property, the burgeoning field of the internet of things (IoT), neighborhood micro-grids, regulatory compliance, identity protection, food safety, law enforcement, property management, land title security, cybersecurity, and bourses from art to coins to public stocks.

The reality of the future of blockchain technology is the mighty disruption of commission-based business models that derive income from fear, uncertainty, and distrust. So called "garbage" fees associated with major purchases like homes and cars will be reduced dramatically by introducing blockchain accountability to these activities. Consumers will win and usury fee dependents will lose in this coming scenario that makes "middlemen" obsolete and unnecessary.

"It's only when you hitch your wagon to something larger than yourself that you will realize your true potential."

President Barack Obama

Chapter 6

Executing the Vision

"Leadership is the capacity to translate vision into reality."

Warren G. Bennis

The most important thing to understand when setting out to take actions that result in successfully executing a vision is that you are not alone in this endeavor. The more people who are recruited to execute a particular vision, the more positive reinforcement the solution will have. It is important that the execution team includes those with personal resources to commit or with the authority to commit public resources.

Execution is not the most entertaining part of building an enterprise. In many ways execution is the process of taking that which was conceived outside of the box and putting it into a box to achieve the necessary conditions of repeatability and exemplary quality in delivering products and services. That said, execution is the lone distinguishing factor separating success from failure in aspiring entrepreneurs. It is also the time in a business life cycle that is most frustrating to creative personalities; this is the Waterloo of many inventors who transition into entrepreneurship.

Beware of the Shiny Objects

The biggest enemy of a good idea in the execution stage is the propensity of inventors and entrepreneurs to succumb to the siren song of another idea that is thought to be bigger, better, and hold more potential than the one that is already poised for success. Business coaches and mentors all deal with entrepreneurs who fall victim to "getting distracted by new shiny objects," the way a fish always seems to get caught by a new lure. It seems to be the nature of inventors and entrepreneurs to enthusiastically chase shiny objects when faced with the prospect of the real work involved in making that last shiny object into a repeatable, profitable business model.

Productivity is important in the execution phase, but productivity often gets confused with activity. During this time, new people are integrated into the efforts and meetings often consume extensive amounts of time. Being busy is not the same as being productive and moving the execution process forward. It is easy to fall into the trap of putting in endless hours dwelling on minutia, or sitting in meetings recycling the same problems and topics day after day. It is important to make every moment add value; that is seldom done in group meetings.

Whether the task at hand is proving that an already proven concept is scalable or evaluating what price the market will pay for a good or service, execution of the task at hand along a well-thought-out plan is vital to your future success. The keys to executing anything, from expanding a start-up business into production or advocating actively for a region to make solid long-term economic decisions, are always the same. They are choosing the right people to work together to move things forward, and maintaining the support and encouragement of influential leaders. Choose your team wisely for competence, attitude, and positivity.

Team Building

Building a capable team to turn visions into reality is a more formidable task than most people realize. An overwhelming majority of those who want to be on a high-performance team are not really cut out to achieve happiness in the environment that true high performance requires. Leading a high-performance team requires diligence, vision, clarity of communication, self-sacrifice, knowledge, energy, a willingness to go the extra mile, and most importantly the knowledge of what you do not know coupled with appreciation for those who do.

There is no room on a high performance team for anyone who undermines the mission of the organization. Undermining a mission can take many forms and should not be confused with offering candid competent criticisms for positive purposes. Undermining can be as simple as being the office "Eeyore," the lovable negative donkey from Winnie the Pooh, who always has a negative outlook on everything. Contrast Eeyore with Tigger, his counterpart in the Hundred Acre Wood, who was so energetic and outwardly positive that real criticisms couldn't faze him. Eeyore and Tigger of course combine to provide classic manic-depressive signals to Pooh, who really just wants more honey. While people like Tigger will always provide a rush of energy and Eeyore will dampen the spirit of any organization, high-performance teams have no place for extreme demeanors. Solid, competent, high-energy people make things happen. These are the skills and demeanors to seek when building a high-performance team.

It is important to fill every role with adequate talent in order to separate tasks and have them completed in a timely manner. Redundancy in staffing only serves to promote discourse. Hire the team that is needed, and not a single person above that. Hire carefully and seldom, but nurture high performers like gold. Your business and your freedom to live outside the box both depend on it.

Cultivating an Atmosphere of Accomplishment

In management publications, much attention has been paid to creating and cultivating an atmosphere of accomplishment. Execution depends on accomplishment, and accomplishment depends on clear goals for each individual. It is most important for those in leadership positions to acknowledge the successful accomplishments of high-performance people. Such team members seek goals and like having them, but they also appreciate being praised and acknowledged for their accomplishments.

Most Americans – including American workers – agree that freedom is valuable and distinguishes us from other cultures.

Living Outside the Box

But allowing performers to exercise autonomy in carrying out their duties is a perk that few businesses offer here in the land of the free. Most organizations are structured to operate inside the box of hourly reporting, precise job descriptions, restrictions on where and how to work, and even valuing process over results. For high-performance people this kind of atmosphere can be toxic: feeling more like Pandora's Box than the box of conformity that most workplaces have put into place. Giving valuable performers the freedom to balance life and work is key to building a high performance team that is continually focused on execution.

Ideas and Ad Hoc Activities are Still Valuable

In each of the last four years that I have served as the CEO of CVEP, the most impactful internal actions were not in our budget or on our task list when we began our fiscal year. This includes the establishment of the Palm Springs Accelerator Campus, the way it was financed, the decision of the Palm Desert City Council to fund a digital iHub in 2019 and even in being included in the Wells Fargo IN2 incubation program as a charter member. All of these things were opportunities that were recognized due to the heightened sense of awareness that the staff has developed. The point here is that a high-performance team should be given license to bring forth opportunities for consideration whenever they are recognized. They will reward you with great execution, enhanced revenue, and more efficiency for granting them this kind of freedom.

Living Outside the Box

Results over Processes

The final advice offered to promote execution of goals is to maintain focus on results as opposed to processes. Results-oriented performers will go to a big box retailer and bring back a hammer for $30 in less than a half hour. A process-driven federal purchasing agent who is following their prescribed orders will get you the same hammer in 60 days at an often-reported price of $700. This example illustrates clearly why a results-oriented atmosphere is almost always superior to a process-driven workplace when something has to get done on a budget and in a timely manner.

In closing, execution depends on deliberate focused action, and that depends on valuing results over process. Only in high-volume manufacturing or well-established medical procedures should process be valued above results, and that is just because the processes are in place to assure repeatability in the results they deliver.

"Vision without execution is hallucination."

Thomas Edison

Living Outside the Box

Living Outside the Box

Chapter 7

Poised for Opportunity

"Unfortunately, there seems to be far more opportunity out there than ability.... We should remember that good fortune often happens when opportunity meets with preparation."

Thomas A. Edison

A plethora of opportunities are never recognized by people who could otherwise have benefitted from them. It is said that opportunity only knocks once but the reality is that opportunity does not knock at all; opportunity is just there, and there are two ways to easily miss out on what life freely makes available. The first way to miss out on an opportunity is to fail to recognize it for what it is. The first reason is unfortunate, but the second is the most tragic. The second reason people miss out on the fruits of opportunity is the fact that they do see the value in a particular opportunity but fail to act on it. Sometimes failure to act is out of fear, while at other times it is due to personal obligations that would make pursuit of opportunity difficult.

Enhancing the ability to recognize more of the opportunities that come into our lives is the subject of this chapter. The first step in seeing opportunities is recognizing the value in the things and situations that are all around us. This goes beyond awareness or recognizing the dots or even connecting them. Instead, it takes a commitment to actualizing the entire set of tasks: from recognition, to vetting, to proof of concept, and through to proof of markets. If all of this can be done, then it is time to consider starting a business or a movement around the identified opportunity.

Opportunity vs. Opportunist

Before getting deeper into being poised for opportunity, it is important to point out the difference between acting on an opportunity and simply being an opportunist. Capitalizing on an opportunity involves living a life of awareness, recognizing an opportunity and then doing the hard work that it takes to truly create commercial success from an idea. On the other hand, opportunists recognize the value of other people's work and concoct schemes to capitalize on other people's efforts or failures. In the animal kingdom, opportunists are called predators, or even scavengers.

In the animal kingdom, scavengers feed on the dead. In business, "investors of last resort" are often referred to as scavengers, swooping in when a business model has been weakened by a well-meaning steward. In life and in the animal kingdom, scavengers are a necessary part of the ecosystem, but scavenging is not the focus of living outside the box, and is not the way to be poised for opportunity.

As opposed to scavengers, who feed on the dead, predators create opportunity at the expense of the weak. Humans admire animal predators for their strength and speed, as evidenced by our affection for jungle cats, wolves, and other predators. *Living Outside the Box* is meant to inspire the opportunities of earned recognition followed by deliberate action. Being aware of the presence of predators and scavengers is an enhanced way to avoid feeding the scavengers with your intellectual property.

Opportunities that Benefit

Economic development agencies typically exist for the sole purpose of fulfilling the mission set forth by its stakeholders. An exemplary mission is to improve, diversify, and desensitize the economy of a particular region.

With a focus that has shifted strongly towards advancing entrepreneurship, CVEP chooses carefully those actions that foster thriving wages in business sectors that are not directly dependent on the region's cyclical tourism-based economy. Thus, when we evaluate applications submitted to the Innovation Hub, the focus is on those businesses whose ideas have the potential to benefit the entire region in a way that furthers our economic goals.

In order to elevate the employment opportunities and wages in the Greater Palm Springs, we must dedicate our resources to assisting business that project high-wage job creation, and we are not interested in assisting businesses that maintain the low-wage status quo. Our historical acceptance rate is somewhat less than 20% of the inquiries that we receive, though we do interview most of the applicants and wish them all well. There are many aspiring entrepreneurs who come to the iHub with ideas that may have business merit but are not likely to ever generate employment. One example of this type of business would be a drop-ship company with no intellectual property, intending to profit from buying low and selling high in online marketplaces with no employees. This has become prevalent in the last decade as platforms like Ebay and Amazon have made reselling easy and lucrative. This is not our target market.

Ideal Entrepreneurs

An ideal aspiring entrepreneur is one that has an idea that addresses an understandable market need in a way that can be proven or disproven at the concept level relatively quickly. Secondly, the entrepreneur and/or the management team should understand the technology and markets associated with their idea, and he or she preferably is capable of applying for and being granted a patent to protect their space in the marketplace. Finally, we encourage a commitment to strongly consider establishing a headquarters or branch office in our region so that the fruits of their labor and our mentorship are rewarded by elevating the local economy.

Some other desirable attributes are a willingness to accept coaching and an open mind about seeking financing for an expansion someday. There is nothing more frustrating than an entrepreneur that becomes their own worst enemy in the financing process.

To a lesser extent, CVEP seeks entrepreneurs with communication skills who are willing to advocate for the programs that we operate as positive catalyst for their success. We take on companies that we believe we can help with expertise in engineering, operations, product development, negotiations, marketing, or finance.

Recognizing and capturing the rewards associated with day-to-day opportunities is much more than just awareness: it is also a mindset that is thoughtful, considerate, open, transparent, and aggressive all at the same time.

Being ready to capitalize on opportunities also requires being in the kind of physical condition that is consistent with being able to work for extended periods of time without getting sick or suffering from fatigue. This does not mean that a successful entrepreneur needs to be in Olympic condition, but it does mean that being in sufficient condition to work 12 to 16 hours per day for months on end is necessary. Enthusiasm can propel you in the early days of a venture to stay the course and work incredible numbers of hours, but to really push an idea through to commercial success will eventually require working when tired and mentally fatigued. We do not test our aspiring entrepreneurs in endurance events, but we do make it abundantly clear that entrepreneurship is not for the faint of heart, the lazy, or people with limited work ethics. Entrepreneurship is not an ideal career path for somebody who watches the clock while they work.

Helpful Stewardship

While having a helpful demeanor is not something that is often addressed as a key to success in business, I have observed that some of the best entrepreneurs are also people who are enthusiastic to help elevate others through coaching, teaching, or sharing of assets. At the Palm Springs Accelerator Campus, the companies in residence borrow equipment from each other and seek each other's counsel on a regular basis. One of our resident clients has a small printed circuit board factory as part of the operation. This company, EV Enterprises, has become the preferred provider of printed circuit boards to all of the companies in the iHub program who have a need for printed circuit boards. It is also ironic that in an atmosphere where California has a reputation for losing such businesses, EV Enterprises moved to Palm Springs from Arizona to take advantage of our programs and the proximity to the massive customer base of Southern California. It is this entrepreneur's willingness and ability to serve that has earned several much-needed revenue-producing jobs as their own products are being launched. Through serving others, EV Enterprises has enjoyed success and in turn has helped other entrepreneurs share in their success.

Core competency is required to be poised for success in any industry. Businesses are at risk when entrepreneurs' depth of knowledge is not sufficient to develop an ideal business model for their product or service.

Living Outside the Box

Starting a business with a well-vetted idea that has outside believers is exciting. Running out of cash without proving a concept is not. The space between proving a concept and a full-fledged product launch is often referred to as the "valley of death." This is when the concept seems to work and a few customers have bought, but going forward requires outside investment. This is the most critical phase of all businesses and is typically when an enterprise grows too large for the founders to manage but too small to hire critical management staff, such as a chief financial officer, a chief operating officer, and professional management. Though it seems counterintuitive, most entrepreneurs are not well-suited to manage their businesses through this phase.

For enterprises that have consumer products that retail for between $20 and $50, the valley of death is the period from reaching an annualized sales rate of $1 million until the sales rate reaches $10 million. Often the profits are higher when the sales are $1 million than they are at $10 million due to the need to bring on people and invest in inventory. This stage of any business is critical, and operating skills become more important to sustained success than either the idea or the charisma of the entrepreneur. This is often the period during which facilities are expanded and distribution contracts are established. Cash flow is high, both on the revenue and expense side, and it takes nearly perfect cash management to navigate through. Easing this transition by mitigating some of the risks associated with expansion is why the Palm Springs Accelerator Campus was established. With this campus we are able to keep our client entrepreneurs from having to sign long-term, personally-guaranteed leases. It also enables us to coach them for a few more years as operations and marketing teams are brought into the company to add structure and sustainability.

In the next chapter we discuss how to maintain an eye on what is going on at the edge of technological developments. Maintaining absolutely current knowledge about advancements in technology enables us to help our client companies and to make good judgments as we advise the leaders of the Coachella Valley. The edge also keeps us personally engaged with the momentum and direction of the global business world, which makes us all very interesting party guests.

Living Outside the Box

Living Outside the Box

Chapter 8

Keepers of the Edge

"However ordinary each of us may seem, we are all in some way special, and can do things that are extraordinary, perhaps until then...even thought to be impossible."

Sir Roger Bannister

Scientists once asserted that no human being could ever run a mile in less than 4 minutes. Many of the Olympic-class runners of the early 1950's came close to breaking the four minute mile, but it was Sir Roger Bannister who first achieved this feat in 1954. Since May 4, 1954, when Sir Bannister pushed the edge of human endurance below the previously-thought impossible barrier, the four-minute mark has been broken by over 1,400 male athletes, and is now the standard of all male professional middle distance runners. In the 64 years since, the mile record has been lowered by almost 17 seconds, and currently stands at 3:43.13. Sir Roger Bannister lived his life outside the box and at the edge of human limitations. He was also a consummate gentleman. He became a legend in track and field, and lived to see many humans run a mile even faster.

"The edge" is defined as the outside limit of an object, area, or surface, or, a place or part furthest away from the center. When it comes to technology, being at the leading edge refers to pushing beyond the distinction of "state-of-the-art". Working at the edge of technology is not for the faint of heart; it is for those who aspire to change the world through innovation, deliberately exceeding the currently accepted limits of humanity. The edge is not a place or a thing that can be touched or associated with an address. The edge is dynamic. It is always in motion: the motion of humanity's endless quest to push the envelope of constraint beyond where it is today. Like the four minute mile, the edge beckons to be pushed further.

Every profession, hobby, and skillset has an edge, where people who aspire to change to world will push past. Pushing the edge in technology, for example, improves the day-to-day lives of people all across the globe. Innovations from the edge have enabled the life expectancy in the poorest countries in 2019 to exceed the life expectancies of the richest countries 200 years ago by a full nine years.

This region has found a comfortable role to play by providing hospitality and entertainment to tourists and snowbirds (people from cold climates that have second homes in the desert). An unfortunate repercussion of this winter-based tourism is the fact that the primary employment in the region cycles up in winter and down in summer. Our hospitality industry, like our decision to pursue renewable energy with our early entrepreneurial support efforts, was driven by the delightful sunny weather that we all enjoy. In the past, pushing past the edge would have involved making investments into a potential hospitality industry. However, today our primary economic drivers are cyclical and offer relatively low wages to most of their employees.

Living Outside the Box

My staff and I have assumed the role of "Keepers of the Edge" for Greater Palm Springs and the Coachella Valley. Our role in elevating the local economy is understanding where companies can push past the edge, without being as subject to seasonal business cycles. It is even possible that some of the innovations from the edge will be adopted by the hospitality industry, elevating their services to a new level and making their business models more profitable. The Coachella Valley has the potential to become a premier testing ground for hospitality-focused innovation.

Automation Trends and Impacts on Employment

In 2017 the McKinsey Global Institute published a study on the coming impacts of automation on jobs and wages. Automation, whether in the automotive industry or other assembly-driven business, has always increased and elevated the overall employment and wage numbers. Historically, for every 100 assembly line employees who lost their jobs to robots, another 110 have been hired into better-paying and higher-skill jobs created by the need for maintenance, upgrades, and by the expanding robotics market. These numbers can be misleading, however. Out of the 100 people who lost their jobs, only a small fraction will be able to transition to the 110 higher-paying jobs. The vast majority of the displaced workers from routine assembly work eventually end up in lesser paying jobs that are much less stable than factory work has been.

There are many people who are left behind because they do not develop the skills necessary for the newly created jobs.

Living Outside the Box

Geographically, automation often ends up displacing jobs from one location to another, further stranding those who lose their jobs in cities and towns that are not participating in the automation boom.

This played out dramatically in the Midwest, when auto plants were shuttered, as were their tier two supply chain partners. When the plants opened elsewhere they were typically in right-to-work states with attractive electrical rates and lower costs of living. Towns like Youngstown, Rochester, Detroit, Flint, Cleveland, Buffalo, Milwaukee, and St. Louis were among the losers. These cities have actually seen population losses over the past several decades with the rise in automation, and suffered corresponding reductions in the tax base. The people who adapted to the new reality relocated for better jobs.

The preferred response to automation, clearly, is to become part of the elevation that leads to better jobs and higher wages.

Benefitting from the inevitable onslaught of automation is a challenge that will need to be addressed in the coming decade in the Coachella Valley. Over 50% of the jobs in our region are in business sectors that the McKinsey Global Institute projects to be dramatically impacted by automation. The largest employers in the Coachella Valley are the hospitality, food services, and retail industries. These industries include physical work, office support, and low-skill services, all of which are expected to be fully automated in the near future.

It is feasible that the Coachella Valley could experience a loss of current employment levels of over 100,000 people by 2030 if the McKinsey study turns out to be accurate. These are likely to be middle-aged workers with families. Failing to address the coming automation displacements could be devastating to the region's unemployment rate.

It must be noted that McKinsey does not predict that the industries whose employment levels are projected to be impacted by automation will suffer degradation of their business models. To the contrary, with labor being one of the highest expenses associated with service industries, our hotel, restaurant, and retail sectors may well increase their earnings significantly as they shed employees.

As an example of how fast automation has impacted one type of highly visible, low-skill service job, we can examine the adoption of fast food kiosks. McDonald's announced in the summer of 2018 that they would install kiosks in 1,000 locations per quarter until completing the conversion to kiosks by 2020. According to Statista, there are just over 14,000 McDonald's locations in the United States. McDonald's is the seventh-largest private employer in the United States, with approximately 375,000 employees. If each McDonald's eliminates 5 employees with kiosks the loss of employment will amount to nearly 70,000 jobs, or 18% of the company's workforce.

According to McDonald's analysis on the first round of kiosks, people tend to order more from the kiosks, the kiosks do not make mistakes, nor do the kiosks draw a wage or benefits, get sick, eat the profits, or steal. Kiosks cost between $3,000 and $10,000 each to install and have very low operational expenses.

Living Outside the Box

Assuming that an entry level fast food worker costs McDonald's $15 per hour with benefits, the break-even time for a kiosk is between 200 and 650 hours. The annualized return on investment for installing kiosks is more than 300%. The reality is that the financial incentive to adopt kiosks is so overwhelming, businesses that fail to do so will be at a serious competitive disadvantage that could put them into bankruptcy.

The innovations that come with automation in other service industries will be just as necessary for cost-effective operation as the kiosks have been to the fast food industry.

It is important to closely monitor development efforts that will impact the local work force. These innovations include robotic bartenders, automated bed changing, industrial cleaning devices, robotic landscaping, driverless delivery, automated food preparation, and online education.

On the flip side, drones like the prototype program in Reykjavik, Iceland using Chinese Aha drones to deliver coffee and other treats will create additional profit centers for food service providers and drone technology professionals. Uber eats will suffer because the early results indicate the drones can make deliveries at 3 times the rate of drivers.

If a region is facing a displacement of as much as 50% of its workforce, the question is: what is to become of these workers? In the Midwest, three things typically happened when automation changed manufacturing. First, some people learned a new skill. These people were free to relocate for a better job or even to use that skill in a different work environment without relocating. Second, there were people who did not elevate their skills, who were not willing to relocate. These people usually accepted lower-wage jobs in exchange for staying in their homes. That option may not exist in future disruptions. The third option is to essentially drop out of the workforce, either surviving on the social safety net or participating in off-the-books labor by doing odd jobs for cash.

The challenge is to find ways to create jobs that are less susceptible to automation, and that pay a thriving wage. The McKinsey Global Institute's three top-growth business sectors are technology professionals, healthcare workers, and builders. All of these are projected to grow by more than 30% by 2030. Additionally, the teaching profession, corporate executives, and creative activities are job sectors projected to grow by roughly 10% over the same time period.

The chosen solutions must allow for employment opportunities in these high growth sectors, so that displaced workers can have a chance at elevating their careers. You can further enhance your chances for future prosperity by advocating now for the digital infrastructure and transportation opportunities necessary to become a preferred location for telecommuters.

Communication Platform Deployment

Communicating effectively and promptly is one of the most important skills in business and government operations. In today's day and age, it is vital for people and businesses alike to have access to the digital infrastructure necessary, in order to communicate, promote distributed workforces, and provide services from a distance.

The most important communication platforms that cities, towns, businesses and citizens rely on are cellular phones and the internet. Both of these platforms are dependent on connection speed and strength. Having an internet connection alone is not sufficient: comparing a low-speed connection to a state-of-the-art service is more drastic than comparing a horse to a commercial airliner.

According to Nate Silver's 538 analysis, Sauguache County, Colorado has the distinction of having the worst internet service in the United States. Unsurprisingly, it is rural and remote. Rural areas not only miss out on the employment opportunities associated with state-of-the-art bandwidth, they can't even access leading edge healthcare that telemedicine makes available. The broadband map of the United States is nearly a perfect indicator of where the high-paying jobs are located. Opportunity follows bandwidth, and bandwidth follows investment. The cycle of haves and have-nots in modern America is fueled by where broadband is deployed and where it is not.

It must be noted that the national providers of bandwidth typically advertise the available download speed, and not the upload speed. In cases where data with high levels of video content needs to be uploaded, upload speed is extremely important. Upload speeds tend to be 10 times slower than download speeds; this becomes quite critical in where digital businesses choose to locate or are able to grow. As you become advocates for increasing the speed and reach of bandwidth offerings it is necessary to continue to emphasize that both download speed and upload speeds are important to businesses.

Cellular phone service has been adopted across the United States over the last several decades. There are currently more than 300 million cell phone accounts in the nation which has only 330 million people. It is accurate to conclude that we have more cell phones that we have adults. However, this does not mean that everyone has cell phone coverage. The nagging reality when it comes to cellular coverage is that there are still large areas of the United States that do not have any reliable cellular coverage. Regions with no coverage or coverage that is limited to voice only cannot benefit from data transfer via cell phones and are essentially handicapped when it comes to communication over cellular networks. Landlines like the ones that were ubiquitous prior to the 1980s are still necessary in these underserved areas.

Another pressing issue involves the dead zones within otherwise well-covered areas. For example, my home is in a dead zone in a community that has otherwise very good coverage. This problem was solved by investing $200 in a booster device that allows us to use our cell phones inside our home. Prior to investing in this booster, we had to go to the far corner of the back yard to get a usable signal. This was not a great experience when the summer heat exceeded 105 degrees. My local representative for our cellular provider tells me that our neighborhood will have coverage sometime in 2019; when that happens, the booster may end up on Ebay.

Most modern automobiles have hands-free cellular capability, so driving is now a time to catch up on calls. It is difficult to drive a distance of over 15 miles without encountering a dead zone which causes calls to be dropped.

As uninterrupted cellular coverage with adequate capacity is critical to business communications, it is important to advocate for continuously upgrading the services offered in the region. The final critical factor with cellular phone coverage is just what kind of coverage is offered. The implementation of many embodiments of the Internet of Things (IoT) will require 5G cellular service. 5G is being rolled out in some cities across the country now and is expected to start to displace 4G widely in 2020. The advantage of 5G is better coverage at higher data transfer speeds. The highest data transfer rates for 4G coverage is on the order of 1 Gbps. This is fast, but the reliability of that speed is location-dependent and degrades rapidly at increased distances from the source. 5G, on the other hand, has been tested at speeds up to 20 Gbps and in theory is believed to be capable of speeds of up to 100 Gbps.

Communications, Cybersecurity and Self Driving Cars

Someday self-driving cars will be widely adopted. These cars will need to be able to communicate with each other and with traffic control in the cloud, and that makes continuous coverage vital. A "dropped call" could mean a wreck, and you could be the passenger. Additionally the continuous communication needs to be secure so a hacker can't hijack the car you are riding in, demanding ransom in exchange for not crashing you into a tree or another car. Locations without continuous coverage and sufficient bandwidth to provide cybersecurity will miss out on the benefits of this innovation.

Implementing 5G requires that repeater boxes need to be placed roughly 1,000 feet apart, as opposed to 4G repeaters which can maintain coverage at up to 10 miles apart. This will be a time-consuming and expensive project, but the Coachella Valley will reap the benefits if we are among the first regions to be covered.

The other compelling reason to advocate for the rapid adoption of 5G coverage is that implementing it will solve the region's bandwidth problem. CVEP will continue to keep our fingers on the pulse of the state of 5G as a way to proverbially kill two birds with one stone.

Living Outside the Box

Working Remotely

Cities on the fringe of mega-cities offer businesses access to tens of millions of potential customers by car. Lifestyles in suburbia are more relaxing and costs of living are also much lower. The vibe of places like Palm Springs or Thousand Oaks are much more coastal-feeling than other inland regions of California, making them appealing to people who are fed up with the coast's cost of living and oppressive commutes. Additionally, these locations are appealing to tech workers currently based in Silicon Valley, where starter homes are over $1 million and the quality of life has degraded due to travel times, homelessness, and crowded entertainment venues.

As a former Bay Area resident who left to start a family, I can attest to Greater Palm Springs' ability to provide the career advantages of the big leading-edge cites, but in a lower-cost place with a higher quality of life. However, there is difficulty to be found in trying to work remotely from an area with insufficient digital infrastructure and a limited number of like-minded tech workers nearby.

Silicon Valley and coastal businesses offer branch offices and employment opportunities in other locations, in order to stay at the leading edge of product development. Of the 20+ locations that Google has established as outposts for remote workers, all of them are located near universities that offer STEM degrees. This trend of moving away from the central headquarters to locations that are capable of keeping the worker efficiencies at coastal levels, all while offering an attractive lifestyle, is something that aspiring branch office locations would be well served to laser-focus on.

The Future of Shopping

Amazon has disrupted the sales and distribution of consumer goods in a way that no one, perhaps with the exception of a few futurists, could have predicted. They have initiated a service where anyone with internet access can buy almost any item without leaving the couch. Orders placed with Amazon, whether books, cleaning supplies, razors, car parts, or even clothing can be expected to be delivered within 48 hours. Amazon is even dabbling with offering groceries and has acquired the Whole Foods markets. Returns are easy too, meaning size-dependent items like shoes can be bought online now.

Amazon has even opened some stores that have no employees called Amazon Go. Shopping at Amazon Go involves using a smartphone to scan and pay for items. No clerks are needed. Much like what kiosks have done to the fast food workers, Amazon Go or other businesses which adopt the electronic brick-and-mortar business model will render in-person service providers obsolete.

Regions that are dependent on retail shopping for a substantial level of taxes and employment are particularly vulnerable to online shopping from Amazon and others, which have disrupted the traditional business model of face-to-face shopping.

Paying close attention to the transition of brick-and-mortar shopping as it morphs into a new model that involves both stores and online offerings is important for retail dependent locations.

Telemedicine

With our 4 regional hospitals and our large number of retirees, including snowbirds, the Coachella Valley has the demographic necessary for medical advances in the field of aging. We also have a large number of people who have a primary care physician elsewhere, sometimes in another country entirely.

This region would benefit from having medical experts located in the area who are also able to provide their patients with services from afar; the field of telemedicine has a lot of potential. Residents and visitors alike would benefit from seeking second opinions from medical professionals elsewhere, and quick access to medical records is extremely important. The McKinsey Global Institute identified healthcare providers as one of the few high growth business clusters that is not particularly sensitive to automation. Incorporating telemedicine into our region is dependent on gaining access to high speed communication like broadband and 5G.

Deliberate Awareness and Analytics

CVEP's acceptance of the tasks associated with being the "Keepers of the Edge" is an exercise in targeted deliberate awareness, recognizing the dots, and connecting them in a way that increases the potential for the region we serve. Utilizing our

Living Outside the Box

GIS technology and other techniques, we continually strive to gather and analyze as much data as possible to identify trends and technologies that are either opportunities to take advantage of, or consequences to avoid. We then aggregate and publish the results of these analyses so that everyone in the Greater Palm Springs region has the opportunity to understand what is going on in the world and how it may impact our region.

While being a "Keeper of the Edge" involves awareness, it is more than simply observing and being aware. Being a competent "Keeper of the Edge" is a task that is simultaneously interesting and energizing, and dependent on constant diligence and advancement. It is one thing to know that automation is coming. But it is another to craft strategies to avoid the negative impacts and to garner support to poise a region to capitalize on the opportunities that automation might provide.

In the next chapter we discuss a high-potential partnership that addresses many of the shortcomings that CVEP pointed out in the 2017 Economic Summit. The creation of this partnership involved both thinking and living outside of the box.

"The best way to predict the future is to create it"

Abraham Lincoln

Living Outside the Box

Chapter 9

Tech-Based Innovation Hubs in the Desert

"People are always blaming their circumstances for what they are. I don't believe in circumstances. The people who get on in this world are the people who get up and look for the circumstances they want, and if they can't find them, make them."

George Bernard Shaw

In 2011, the State of California and the City of Palm Springs signed an agreement that created six innovation hubs called iHubs. The Palm Springs iHub was encouraged to specialize in renewable energy technologies since the greater Palm Springs region is a perfect location for sun and wind. During our first six years of operation we accepted 70 companies into the program, and are still mentoring 36 of them.

Renewable energy is not a business cluster that typically needs high levels of bandwidth, so in the early years of operation bandwidth was not an issue. As the companies applying for admission began to move towards increasingly data-driven businesses in the fields of health and medical technology, geographic information systems, broadcasting, blockchain and the internet of things, bandwidth became a critical path problem. Little did we know what would come about when we exposed the Coachella Valley's bandwidth shortcomings at the 2017 Economic Summit.

Amazon Requirements as a Catalyst

In the early fall of 2017, Amazon shocked the nation by announcing that they would be establishing a second headquarters away from their Seattle location. Economic development agencies across the country downloaded the Amazon RFP and started poring over it in preparation to secure the new complex that became known as HQ2.

Here in Greater Palm Springs, The Desert Sun newspaper got on the bandwagon and published an article about why the Coachella Valley would be the ideal location for HQ2. Our sunshine, quality of life, relatively low-cost housing, proximity to the logistical center of the Inland Empire, and short commuting times were all touted as advantages that could be leveraged to attract Amazon to town. It was even mentioned that Amazon CEO Jeff Bezos loves to visit.

As the CEO of CVEP, the regional entity charged with business attraction, I also downloaded the HQ2 RFP and to see exactly what Amazon was looking for in a second headquarters. After reviewing the RFP it was clear to me that the Coachella Valley did not meet the basic requirements set forth by Amazon. I was subsequently interviewed by The Desert Sun in a follow up article titled "Here's all the reasons why the Coachella Valley won't become Amazon's new headquarters." The follow-up article went point-by-point through the requirements that were set forth in Amazon's RFP, and addressed our shortcomings one by one.

The first requirement in the Amazon proposal was a minimum population of 1 million people within 30 minutes of HQ2. With a population of only 460,000 in the Coachella Valley, this requirement alone took us off of the table. Mr. Bezos was not likely to be swayed by the fact that we are projected to grow to that level by 2050.

Our region could not deliver on the second requirement, either: the bandwidth to support an engineering team of 50,000 employees. The RFP even pointed out that if one can't watch a movie on Netflix without losing the signal that serving a giant technology development company with 50,000 employees was out of the question for now.

Amazon expressed a requirement for HQ2 to be near an international airport with daily direct flights to San Jose, Seattle, New York City and Washington, DC. Palm Springs International Airport has regular flights to Seattle and the Bay Area. However, it only offers seasonal flights to New York and has never offered direct flights to the nation's capital.

Amazon also included a requirement to be close to a major university system that can supply graduates in fields like computer science, engineering and finance. At the time the public university in the Coachella Valley only offered nursing degrees on campus with plans to someday offer a business degree with a specialty in hospitality. The current state of affairs

114

in advanced education did not address Amazon's stated requirements.

Another obstacle was Amazon's stated expectation of a massive incentive package. Amazon was already advising interested bidders that incentives would be part of the decision process, and that the 50,000 jobs and $5 Billion of local investments will merit offers of incentive packages well over a billion dollars. The Coachella Valley, with a relatively small population base of moderate-income people, would never have been able to compete for HQ2 in the basis of incentives.

The final shortcoming was the non-existence of a readily available start-up facility of 500,000 square feet.

The article ended when I did give a ray of hope for future smaller attraction projects for branch offices of the Amazons, Googles, Apples, and Facebooks of the world. But this is possible if and only if we can find a way to supply the required bandwidth, and expand the Palm Desert Campus of California State University San Bernardino to include the STEM degrees that these types of companies all require.

One month before the news of the Amazon HQ2 project, I had an article published in the Valley Voice column of the Desert Sun under the title "Three Wishes for a Prosperous Future for the Coachella Valley." The three wishes were as follows:

Bandwidth

Currently there is no state-of-the-art bandwidth available to businesses and individuals in the Coachella Valley. Presently the state-of-the-art speed of data transfer in research institutions and for high-end users like Google is 100 Gbps. This speed is over 10,000 times faster than the bandwidth in CVEP's main office. To the best of my knowledge, the highest speed fiber available locally is at the CSUSB Palm Desert Campus: that is currently set to 1 Gbps and must be used in a way that serves academic purposes. The Coachella Valley desperately needs to upgrade and maintain its digital infrastructure.

Venture Capital

Startup technology companies are often funded by dollars secured from venture capital firms. Venture capital firms pool investor dollars and deploy those dollars over a period of time into the equity of promising companies with high-growth potential. The Greater Palm Springs region has no venture capital firms. Not a single dollar of the equity investments made into the iHub companies came from a local venture capital fund.

There is sufficient wealth in the valley to merit a venture capital firm with its headquarters here. The wealth-building success of Silicon Valley has largely been achieved through leveraging two things: the talent and financial prowess of the multitude of venture capital firms on Sand Hill Road; and its proximity to world-class universities turning ambitious, talented graduates. Any region that aspires to participate in the financial gains of job creation and equity appreciation needs a home-based venture capital firm.

Higher Education

CSUSB-Palm Desert, UCR Palm Desert Campus, and the College of the Desert are major contributors to the intellectual capital of the Coachella Valley and they should be admired for what they do. What we have now is only the beginning of what we need to supply the workforce of the future. The Coachella Valley desperately needs a future that includes institutes of higher learning offering degrees in business, engineering, chemistry, biology, and the other majors associated with a comprehensive full-service college. These are the degrees that places like Silicon Valley, Austin, and Boston leverage into the creation of wealth from the invention process and entrepreneurship.

The 2017 Economic Summit

These three wishes became the centerpiece of my presentation for the 2017 Economic Summit. The presentation went through the Amazon RFP one requirement at a time. I used graphics to illustrate the winnowing-down of HQ2's 236 suitors, who reportedly spent an average of $250,000 each in an attempt to woo Amazon to town. My presentation also stated with clarity why Greater Palm Springs, wisely, did not waste $250,000 to put together a proposal that would not be remotely competitive. This was the opportunity to carefully set forth the three wishes that I had outlined in my newspaper opinion piece. These three wishes, I explained, will set the stage for the local entrepreneurial community to be able to compete effectively in the knowledge economy. I emphasized again: these ideas should be taken seriously for future attraction opportunities that are compatible with our population, infrastructure and lifestyle.

The results since that time have been phenomenal. The CSUSB-Palm Desert Campus is connected to the CENIC optical fiber line: CENIC connects educational institutions in California ultra-high-speed bandwidth. But while the service has traditionally provided 10Gbps, it is now in the process of upgrading the service to 100Gbps which really is at the leading edge of light. Equally exciting, the campus will be home to a cybersecurity program and a degree in entrepreneurship in the fall of 2019. Cybersecurity at CSUSB-Palm Desert will be the first four-year STEM degree available in the Coachella Valley. The stage is now set for expanding into other STEM programs.

These announcements and associated activities settle the bandwidth issue, at least for those entities that can tie into the CENIC line, which is reserved for universities, public libraries, municipalities, and K-12 schools.

Game-Changing Partnership

After the 2017 Economic Summit, the City of Palm Desert stepped forward and expressed an interest in establishing an innovation hub on the CSUSB-Palm Desert Campus that would seek to attract entrepreneurs in the digital space. When it was revealed that a cybersecurity program was being considered for the campus, the idea for a partnership was formed.

Living Outside the Box

In the fall of 2018 it was announced at the CVEP 2018 Economic Summit that a partnership had been formed between the City of Palm Desert, CVEP, and CSUSB to establish a digital iHub that has access to the CENIC fiber. In a single year, the combination of awareness, vision and willingness to work together has resulted in the two most important of the three wishes being granted. At the time of publication, we are looking forward to cutting the ribbon on the Palm Desert Digital iHub in 2019. The new iHub will be home to 100Gbps fiber-based bandwidth, the Comcast MachineQ IoT development platform and both the cybersecurity and entrepreneurship programs of CSUSB-Palm Desert.

This is a perfect example of what can happen when the right people and the right ideas come together in partnership. Standing barriers are quickly removed when action-oriented people are willing to think and live outside the box, resolving to work together to elevate at regional economy.

Our jobs of eternal awareness, serving as keepers of the edge, exposing shortcomings, and calling for actions that improve the economy will never be complete. The Palm Desert Digital iHub, like the Palm Springs iHub before it, is poised to be a catalyst for thriving-wage jobs. They will also become a magnet for workers from Silicon Valley and other high-cost, high-anxiety regions. The Coachella Valley simply offers people a better quality of life.

Prior to the establishment of a high-bandwidth option there were many jobs that simply could not be done in Greater Palm

Springs. The day is coming when there is a large demand for off-campus bandwidth. After seeing the vision of the last year realized, I am confident that the regional stakeholders will find an out-of-the-box way to deliver.

"There are no constraints on the human mind, no walls around the human spirit and no barriers to our progress except those we ourselves erect."

President Ronald Reagan

Living Outside the Box

Chapter 10

People Who Changed the World

This last chapter of Living Outside the Box covers six people who have changed the world by invention, innovation, and commerce. These six all enjoyed financial success as a result of their inventions and suffered ridicule during their lives for living so far outside the box.

In no particular order, here are the stories of people who have changed the world.

Bill Gates

Bill Gates path to entrepreneurial success started as a child when at age 13 he and his friend Paul Allen became interested in computers. They had a natural affinity for computers, and were often exempted from attending class to pursue this passion. Gates, Allen, and two other students wrote a program that was adopted and used by their school for scheduling classes. This was the start of a very productive and wealth-creating adventure.

From the Lakeside School where Gates scored 1,590 out of 1,600 on his SAT, he chose to attend Harvard University where he met the future CEO of Microsoft Steve Ballmer. Gates never had a study plan at Harvard and eventually left without graduating to join Paul Allen at Honeywell, where their passion for programming continued. A year later they started a business called Microsoft; the rest is history.

Bill Gates went on to revolutionize the computer industry by partnering with IBM to develop the operating system that put personal computing within reach of everyday people. While it is widely believed that Gates and his partners invented the operating system, this is not quite true. Gates instead recognized the potential of an existing operating system called SCP, which was not quite ready to be utilized by the public, and through his diligence and hard work created an operating system to reach the masses.

The computing world has never been the same since Microsoft released Windows in 1985. The product suite called Microsoft Office, the produce suite that includes PowerPoint, Word, Excel, and more, has become the dominant software platform for business over the last 30 years. It was Gates' ability to recognize and connect the dots with IBM's business strategies that launched the enterprise empire Microsoft.

Bill Gates' persistence, self-education in early life, and his ability to recognize and act on potential led him to great success.

His life now is spent running one of the richest charitable organizations on the planet, the Bill and Melinda Gates Foundation, which could only have come about through the financial success of Microsoft. The Foundation's mission is to change the world with a philanthropic platform that is laser-focused on efficacious solutions.

"Microsoft was founded with a vision of a computer on every desk, and in every home. We've never wavered from that vision."

Bill Gates

Lee Kuan Yew

Lee Kuan Yew, the founder of modern Singapore, led a mosquito-infested tropical island that began as little more than a British outpost. Lee Kuan Yew, or LKY as he is known, is credited with bringing Singapore from a third-world to a first-world country in just a single generation.

LKY did not support populist policies as a way to transform Singapore; instead, he favored long-term social and economic planning. He championed meritocracy and multiracialism as governing principles, and decreed that English was the common language to integrate its immigrant society and to facilitate trade with the West.

LKY mandated bilingualism in schools to preserve students' mother tongue and ethnic identity. His rule was criticized by western media for curtailing civil liberties, even as Singapore grew to a thriving nation state of over 5 million people of many cultures. He instituted disciplinary measures designed to promote political stability and economic vitality. He also adopted the rule of law as the chosen means of governance.

Living Outside the Box

Some of the instituted punishments are still practiced in Singapore to this day, such as caning and the use of the death penalty. They are likely meant to keep people in line with social norms: encouraging them to live within the box. Perhaps such things were necessary in the past, when this city-state was but a hodgepodge of peoples with no prior history or intention of cooperating with each other. These practices still play an important role in maintaining order, though it is hard to measure to what degree they are still necessary.

Those who have visited Singapore, whether for business or personal reasons, understand just how safe and orderly this city-state is. Walking around at night and travelling by subway is as safe in Singapore as walking in affluent gated neighborhoods in most American cities. Locals and visitors alike can thank LKY for a fear-free standard of living in Singapore. Because of LKY's policies, Singapore has been able to leverage its strategic location to not only become the prime hub for Asian shipping and commerce, but also to attract western manufacturers due to its low cost of production. LKY instituted laws against offensive behaviors, such as spitting, littering, failure to flush public toilets, uncivil conduct and more. These kinds of offenses can result in one being stiffly fined, and this has precipitated a cottage industry in "Singapore is a *Fine* City" merchandise. Other offenses like groping, graffiti, and various forms of defacing public property are punished by caning which is a state-instituted whipping by a civil servant called a flogger.

These punishments have been admonished by the western press as cruel and unusual, but in reality they have worked to create a shining prosperous city out of a disorderly swamp in just a half century. Lee Kuan Yew is an example of awareness, focus, diligence, and perseverance in a region that needed all of the above. He not only lived outside the box but his innovations in governance have provided millions of others with opportunities for a lifestyle that other places similar to early Singapore still do not enjoy.

"If you want to reach your goals and dreams, you cannot do it without discipline."

Lee Kuan Yew

Albert Einstein

Most of us are aware that Dr. Albert Einstein is the person who discovered the famous relationship between energy, mass and the speed of light. He is regarded by many as the smartest man to have lived in the 20th century yet his intelligence quotient (IQ) is only estimated to be 160, which is equaled or exceeded by quite a large number of people. Statistical analysis would put Dr. Einstein four standard deviations above the average human for IQ, which corresponds to 3 in 100,000 people. That seems stratospheric; but to put this in perspective, among the 500,000 people in the Coachella Valley, there should be 15 who are either as smart as or smarter than Einstein. The United States should have 10,000 such people, and the world should have at least 210,000 that fall into this category.

The question then becomes, with so many "Einsteins" on earth why is it that Dr. Albert Einstein came to be regarded so highly? For all of the brilliant mathematical theories that came from the mind of Dr. Einstein, he had a well established reputation for being absent-minded. He was known to forget his own address, to value imagination above science, and even failed (or forgot) to cash his significant check for being named the winner of the Nobel Prize in Physics.

Einstein's personal life was much the same as many others: he had multiple marriages and children with different mothers. He also held jobs of little significance and eventually settled in as a patent examiner after being rejected for a teaching position he had sought for two years. He was not a flashy dresser or a celebrated orator, and with the exception of developing the theory of relativity at a young age, Einstein may well have been like a physics teacher at a community college.

What really set Einstein apart for a person of such brilliance were his interests in many different subjects. He enjoyed music, wine, arts, books, philosophy and, of course, science. Einstein has been chronicled as a welcome guest at parties, and he was good with people. He is also credited with caring little or nothing for celebrity or public officials.

What set Einstein apart from famous scientists of his time and today was his awareness of the dark potential of science and the love for humanity in general. He urged avoidance of nuclear weapons at the highest levels including authoring a letter to the President of the United States on the matter.

Einstein's ability to think outside the box in a field that most people avoid like a cat avoids a bath set him apart. His appreciation for the things that make us human and his humble nature endeared him to the masses. Einstein appreciated and promoted simplicity in a profession that celebrates complexity. For that rare ability to go his own way in a field that is thought to be prohibitively difficult, Albert Einstein will always be the gold standard for intelligence even if there are 210,000 people on earth who could score higher on an IQ test.

"Any intelligent fool can make things bigger and more complex... It takes a touch of genius – and a lot of courage to move in the opposite direction."

Albert Einstein

Leonardo da Vinci

Leonardo da Vinci's IQ has been estimated to be upwards of 220, 60 points above Einstein's- which is already 60 points above the average IQ. Da Vinci's IQ corresponds to only one occurrence in trillions- which gives him the distinction of being possibly the most intelligent person to have ever lived.

Leonardo's curiosity and processing power at such an advanced level stimulated him at a level it would take the average person lifetimes to achieve. Although da Vinci is mostly recognized for his skill as an artist, he also created schematics of advanced inventions like diving bells, submarines, helicopters, and many other items that were not commercialized until over 400 years after his death. Da Vinci's awareness was at a level not seen before or since. His interests were seemingly unlimited, as were his accomplishments in all types of art, science, medicine, machinery, materials, mathematics, literature and more. It is hard to imagine anyone on Earth who might have been more skilled than da Vinci in any task.

Da Vinci's personal life was complicated as it often is with highly important, skilled people. Religious leaders created and enforced rules meant to keep the common person in a small box, living under guidelines that the elite deemed appropriate. At a young age, da Vinci and three of his contemporaries were charged with homosexual acts, but were eventually acquitted. Had he been convicted, his freedom and even his life would have been in jeopardy.

Da Vinci was able to live his life with the financial backing of wealthy patrons of the time such as the Medici family of Italy. Such commissions provided him with the time to visualize fabulous machines of the future, create spectacular – and oftentimes religiously-inspired – pieces of art, and do original research on a vast array of leading-edge techniques. The Medici family's protection certainly came with protection from persecution by religious officials for his uniqueness and preferences.

Da Vinci's name is synonymous with the Renaissance: the period from the 14th to 17th centuries when science came out of the shadows and art flourished. To this day, people with multiple skills are known as Renaissance men. This is the period during which enlightenment began, ushering in the atmosphere that allows people to live outside of the box.

In today's hyper-specialized world, one wonders: would another Leonardo da Vinci be possible?

Living Outside the Box

"Simplicity is the ultimate sophistication"

Leonardo da Vinci

Tim Berners-Lee

The communication available to people and institutions today is only possible because of the invention of the internet. Despite what our former Vice President Al Gore once said, he is not the inventor of the internet. That distinction belongs to Tim Berners-Lee, a professor of computer science at Oxford University and the Massachusetts Institute of Technology (MIT). Unlike Bill Gates and Steve Jobs who did not graduate from college, Berners-Lee completed his studies and graduated with a bachelor's degree in physics.

Much like many young engineers, Berners-Lee spent his early career employed by various goal-oriented companies. During a contracting stint at CERN in Switzerland he proposed a project based on hypertext which eventually became HTTP: the basic language of the internet. The thing that really sets Berners-Lee apart is that he did not become an entrepreneur. Rather than strike out on his own he has always enjoyed the benefit of a regular paycheck from various private and government entities.

Berners-Lee found a way to bring a new and highly impactful technology to the world from the inside of organizations that have typically been averse to risk-taking. For this ability to live outside the box while in the box and for the massive positive impact of the World Wide Web, Sir Timothy Berners-Lee has earned this profile in Living Outside the Box.

"There are billions of neurons in our brains, but what are neurons? Just cells. The brain has no knowledge until connections are made between neurons. All that we know, all that we are, comes from the way our neurons are connected."

Tim Berners-Lee

Steve Jobs

I choose to close this chapter by honoring the life of an innovator who lived outside the box whom I personally was fortunate to have known. During the development of the Macintosh, I was working in the R&D group as a young engineer at Verbatim Corporation in Sunnyvale, California. Verbatim was developing the 3.5 inch floppy disk specifically for the Macintosh and I was peripherally involved in the project, although my primary assignment was designing the world's first 3.5 inch erasable optical disk that eventually became the CD ROM Burner.

Steve would come in many mornings in search of good disks to use in testing the Macintosh. Some days there were no disks that had passed the overnight tests. The metal ring that centered the floppy disks were key to being able to achieve the track density (tpi) needed to enable the Mac to boot up. When he didn't get his disks, Steve would get quite angry, and often cursed about it: sometimes, he got personal. Though most of the people on the team were afraid of him, my rural Kentucky upbringing prepared me well to deal with anger and cussing (that is Kentuckian for cursing). I cussed him back, and he seemed to respect that, so we got along very well.

I never saw Steve again after that project with the exception of the 1985 Super Bowl on Stanford's campus while I was in graduate school there. I tried to crash the Apple tailgate party and was ushered away. Steve was in the distance and smiled at me, seemingly unaware that the bouncer was escorting me out. Since then, I have followed his career and always admired what he was able to achieve in spite of his prickly personality. Here is my salute to my old friend, Steve.

Steven Paul Jobs is one of the most enigmatic personalities to ever grace the stage of American entrepreneurship. He was adopted by a Cupertino (Silicon Valley) couple and grew up less than 5 miles from the current world headquarters of Apple, the company that he and Steve Wozniak founded when they were young and curious about personal computing. He earned a reputation for being demanding and disrespectful from his early days as an innovator in Silicon Valley.

Like Bill Gates, Jobs gave college a try and rejected it as something he saw no value in. He described dropping out of college as one of the best decisions of his life. What he did develop in his brief time in college was an appreciation for calligraphy which led him to incorporate stylish fonts into Apple's Macintosh computers. The stylish fonts and the graphical user interface (GUI) that was developed separately at Xerox Parc, under the tutelage of Dr. Bill Verplank (who was my *Human Factors in Design* professor at Stanford), became the differentiator between Apple and IBM in the personal computer marketplace. Some have said that Jobs' experimentation with hallucinogenic drugs is where this inspiration came from, and others blame it on his headstrong nature.

Like many Silicon Valley wunderkinds, Jobs became very wealthy well before turning 30. By the time he reached the age of 30, Apple was experiencing growing pains and the board of directors brought in a seasoned corporate executive named John Scully to be the adult in the room. In the early days the relationship was outwardly great, but Jobs never really acclimated himself to the ways of the box that corporate America operates in. The pinnacle of the relationship between Jobs and Scully was probably the Apple Super Bowl tailgate party on the Stanford campus in 1985. Shortly after, the blush was off the rose, and Steve was fired from the company he started in his parent's garage.

Jobs went on to found Next and Pixar, both of which were quite successful. After living inside the box did not solve Apple's woes, Steve Jobs was recruited to come back in 1997, bringing his creative persona with him. During his second stint at Apple, Jobs went on to revolutionize the music distribution business model and to become the driving force behind the Apple iPhone. Both of these products were scoffed at by traditionalists and both did what Steve enjoyed most: shoving success into the face of his naysayers. In the summer of 2018 Apple became the first public company to attain a market capitalization of over $1 Trillion. If he had lived, he would have relished this milestone.

Living Outside the Box

Sadly, Steve Jobs passed away in 2011 from pancreatic cancer at the young age of 56. Steve lived with cancer for long enough to reflect on his life, and he gave his most impactful speech to the graduating class of Stanford University in 2005 after being diagnosed. Some of the most inspiring excerpts and a look into the soul of Steve Jobs and his life of Living Outside the Box are below.

"Many people are living a lie, doing what they don't want to do and living someone else's life. Find what you love to do, what you love to do. Not what your parents, siblings, cousins, friends, or boss wants you to do. It's up to you how you choose to live. You have to shape your life the way you want it to be daily so that you can live your life on your own terms."

"Failure is the stepping stone to success, failure teaches us what we need to do better, and it makes us wiser, and helps us grow as an individual. We must heed the lessons of failure so that we may prosper."

"You can't connect the dots looking forward; you can only connect them looking backwards. So you have to trust that the dots will somehow connect in your future. You have to trust in something — your gut, destiny, life, karma, whatever. This approach has never let me down, and it has made all the difference in my life."

"Your time is limited, so don't waste it living someone else's life. Don't be trapped by dogma — which is living with the results of other people's thinking. Don't let the noise of others' opinions drown out your own inner voice. And most important, have the courage to follow your heart and intuition. They somehow already know what you truly want to become. Everything else is secondary."

"Stay hungry and stay foolish"

Steve Jobs

Conclusion

The fundamental assertion of this book is that all significant, world-changing progress has been developed by people who were clever enough to recognize solutions and bold enough to take the risks associated with introducing change. This was just as true in ancient times as it is today. Even when they recognize the potential for adding value, corporate America and governments alike are resistant to changes that will impact their operating models.

If the anthem of entrepreneurial success has a chorus, it would likely be my mantra: "what good is it to think outside of the box if one is not willing to live outside the box?" My desire is to inspire readers to live a life outside the box, elevating their own lives in a way that positively impacts others. I truly hope that a compelling case has been made.

Economic development has not typically been a bastion of creativity. Practitioners of the trade often lean heavily on traditional methods; data and science are often not the primary tools used to elevate regional economies. By taking on the challenge posed by our stakeholders' mission, CVEP is changing the way economic development is done and living far outside of the box that many would impose upon us. If you enjoyed this book, please let CVEP know how it has impacted your outlook on life.

Good luck, good life, and never let fear keep you from achieving the life you desire.

Definitions and References

Definitions

Business Incubator: A business incubator is a company that helps new and startup companies to develop by providing services such as management training or office space. The National Business Incubation Association (NBIA) defines business incubators as a catalyst tool for either regional or national economic development.

Economic Development: The process by which a nation improves the **economic**, political, and social well-being of its people.

Proof of Concept: Evidence, typically derived from an experiment or pilot project, which demonstrates that a design concept, business proposal, etc., is feasible.

Proof of Market: When a proven concept for a product or service culminates in a significant number of purchases of that product or service for their general benefit. Purchases validate the viability of a particular product or service in a free market.

Centralized Planning: An economy primarily based on central planning is referred to as a planned economy. In a centrally planned economy, the allocation of resources is determined by a comprehensive plan of production which specifies output requirements.

Living Outside the Box

Distributed Production: local manufacturing is a form of decentralized manufacturing practiced by enterprises using a network of geographically dispersed manufacturing facilities that are coordinated using information technology.

Supply Chain: A network between a company and its suppliers to produce and distribute a specific product to the final buyer. This network includes different activities, people, entities, information, and resources.

USSR: A socialist state in Eurasia that existed from 30 December 1922 to 26 December 1991. Nominally a union of multiple nations, its government and economy were highly centralized. The country was a one-party state, governed by the Communist Party with Moscow as its capital in its largest republic

Airbnb: A privately held global company headquartered in San Francisco that operates an online marketplace and hospitality service which is accessible via its websites and mobile apps. Members can use the service to arrange or offer lodging, primarily homestays, or tourism experiences.

Uber: A transportation network company headquartered in San Francisco, California. Uber offers services including peer-to-peer ridesharing, ride service hailing, food delivery, and a bicycle-sharing system. The company has operations in 785 metropolitan areas worldwide.

Living Outside the Box

Lyft: A transportation network company based in San Francisco, California and operating in the United States and Canada. It develops, markets, and operates the Lyft mobile app. Launched in June 2012, Lyft operates in approximately 300 U.S. cities, and provides over 1 million rides per day.

Scavenger: Someone who scavenges, especially one who searches through rubbish for food or useful things. In the business world scavengers are those who evaluate distressed businesses for value that is not recognized by others and takes the opportunity to take that value for themselves (aka bottom feeder).

Opportunity: A set of circumstances that makes it possible to do something.

Opportunist: A person who exploits circumstances to gain immediate advantage rather than being guided by consistent principles or plans.

Intellectual Property: a work or invention that is the result of creativity, such as a manuscript or a design, to which one has rights and for which one may apply for a patent, copyright, trademark, etc.

The Edge: pushing the frontier of thought or analysis to the limit of currently accepted thinking and computing processes. Visionaries are often seen as living at the outer edge of life.

Living Outside the Box

The Cloud: cloud computing means storing and accessing data and programs over the Internet instead of your computer's hard drive. The cloud is just a metaphor for the Internet.

Snowbirds: A North American term for a person who migrates from the higher latitudes and colder climates of the northern United States and Canada in the southward direction in winter to warmer locales such as Florida, California, Nevada, Arizona, New Mexico, Texas, or elsewhere along the Sun Belt.

Visionary: A person with original ideas about what the future will or could be like.

Vision: The capacity to envisage future market trends and plan accordingly

References

1. **Satanovsky, Gary**. "John Wanamaker's Store Brings Electric Light." Famous Daily, http://www.famousdaily.com/history/wanamaker-installs-electric-lights-dept-store.html

2. **CVEP Video:** https://cvep.com/2018-cvep-feature-video-back-from-the-future/

3. **Coats, Dennis.** "Growth Effects of Sports Franchises, Stadiums, and Arenas: 15 Years Later." https://www.mercatus.org/publication/growth-effects-sports-franchises-stadiums-and-arenas-15-years-later

4. Hayden, Nichole. "Start-up business accelerator coming to Palm Desert to lure tech entrepreneurs." The Desert Sun, July 5, 2018. https://www.desertsun.com/story/news/2018/07/05/palm-desert-ihub-expected-operational-fall/757033002/

5. Tapscott, Don & Alex. "The Blockchain Revolution."

http://blockchain-revolution.com/

6. **Causey, Michael.** "Anybody got a $1,000 toilet seat."
https://federalnewsnetwork.com/federal-
report/2014/10/anybody-got-a-1000-toilet-seat/

7. **McKinsey Global Institute.** "A Future that Works:
Automation, Employment, and Productivity." 2017
https://www.mckinsey.com/~/media/mckinsey/featured
%20insights/Digital%20Disruption/Harnessing%20auto
mation%20for%20a%20future%20that%20works/MGI-
A-future-that-works-Executive-summary.ashx

8. **Brookings Institute.** "Automation and AI will Disrupt
the American Labor Force. Here's How we can Protect
Workers." **February 2019**
https://www.brookings.edu/blog/the-
avenue/2019/02/25/automation-and-ai-will-disrupt-the-
american-labor-force-heres-how-we-can-protect-
workers/

9. **Mims, Christopher.** "Your Drone Delivered Coffee is
Almost Here." March 30, 2019

Living Outside the Box

https://www.wsj.com/articles/your-drone-delivered-coffee-is-almost-here-11553918415?mod=hp_lead_pos9

10. Malone, Clare. "The Worst Internet in America."
July 27, 2017, 538 Blog.
https://fivethirtyeight.com/features/the-worst-internet-in-america/

11. Wallace, Joe J. "Why I left Silicon Valley." CVEP
website, 2019 https://cvep.com/why-i-left-silicon-valley/

Living Outside the Box

Acknowledgements and Dedications

I am forever grateful to **Laura E. James** for editing this book. She made this book much better through her hard work and a knowledge of the English language that surpasses my own.

My wife **Karen Wallace** was the continual encouragement over the last 10 years while this book was marinating in my mind. She is one of the few people who really knows how to move me to action while avoiding squashing the creative process.

The staff of the **Coachella Valley Economic Partnership** that includes **Laura E. James, Lesa Bodnar, David Robinson, Agustin Aragon, David Robinson, and Patty Clouser** have all provided the inspirations that helped take this concept through its final chapters.

The people of **Sturgis, Kentucky** during my childhood made up the safe and supportive atmosphere that nurtured the courage it took to live outside the box in a world that is not always accepting of people like myself who are from the rural south.

Dr. William O. Hartsaw of the University of Evansville was my advisor and the first person to encourage me to apply to the graduate engineering class of Stanford University.

Cai and Alice Kinberg of Saratoga, CA taught me how to swim like the Swedish and think from a global perspective.

My fellow entrepreneurs **Majeed (Mike) Abed, Al Vaitkus, Ted Watler, Russell Pavlat and the Zygo FHT Division Staff**.

Living Outside the Box

Bowers Holt Wallace and Betty Cain Wallace

My father **Bowers (Rabbit) Wallace** grew up in Sturgis, Kentucky and answered the call of duty to defend our nation in General Patton's Army in World War II. He was captured in the battle of the Volturno River in Cassino, Italy after crossing a bridge that many of his company never crossed. He was transported by train to a POW camp in Mühlberg, Germany where he was a prisoner for roughly two years. One day the guards were gone and the POWs essentially liberated themselves and walked west until they encountered allied troops for transport home. He became the first in his family to graduate from college and spent a distinguished career as a teacher and elementary school principal in Sturgis. He passed away too young in 1992 but his reputation as a model citizen still lives on. He was always amused by my outside the box antics and encouraged them in a quiet compassionate way.

My mother **Betty Cain Wallace** was a child of the depression who spent her early childhood in London, Kentucky under the care of her grandparents and two aunts. She attended school in Lexington and married my dad shortly after his graduation from the University of Kentucky. She embraced Sturgis as her own and lived there until her death in 2018. Most people never realized the level of creativity that she had leading the Sturgis 4H Talent Clubs to multiple state championships. She was in her own way an artist and an inventor. The spicy part of my personality that does not suffer fools or bullies came from her. The peacekeeper and servant in me came from my dad.

Living Outside the Box

Ron H. Cosby

Ron Cosby came into my life at what was possibly one of the most confusing and difficult times that I have had as a professional. About six months after my separation from GAGE where I had seen many practices that were less than in the best interest of the taxpayers by elected officials, may phone rang and it was Ron. Ron was just expanding a local blog called the City County Observer to advocate for good public policy in Vanderburgh County, Indiana. He had a tip for a sneaky yet legal thing that happened while I was CEO of GAGE. The expose' on having a side contract for a city employee at a non-profit was my first of thousands of articles for the City County Observer. My signature appeared on none of the documents because I had refused to sign them. That was part of the rift that lead to my departure.

Later that year, we coined the term SNEGAL to describe actions that are sneaky but legal. Over the next nine years the City County Observer has relentlessly exposed self-serving actions within local government that has financially compromised the taxpayers. Many of the articles were contributed by me and writing them was the best therapy I have ever been paid to engage in.

Ron helped my find my voice at a time that it was fading. He offered unconditional love and friendship when I was down. Without Ron, there would be no living outside the box. I am forever in his debt.

Living Outside the Box

Made in the USA
San Bernardino, CA
18 May 2019